Sally Carter

MEDICINE FROM GOD

Medicine From God
To be kept in the
Prayer Room at all times.

MEDICINE FROM GOD

SCRIPTURE VERSES TO ENCOURAGE
AND COMFORT THE SICK

COMPILED BY
BETH BOSSERMAN

Pleasant Word
A Division of WinePress Group
PW

Pleasant Word (a division of WinePress Publishing, PO Box 428, Enumclaw, WA 98022) functions only as book publisher. As such, the ultimate design, content, editorial accuracy, and views expressed or implied in this work are those of the author.

ISBN 13: 978-1-4141-1473-6
ISBN 10: 1-4141-1473-7
Library of Congress Catalog Card Number: 2009904485

To family and friends who helped me during my illness with cancer. To all of you who ministered to my family while Mark and I took care of Grant. Thank you.

In memory of my precious infant son Grant Nathaniel, who went to be with God on the morning of July 25, 2008. You are my great gift of the Lord.

CONTENTS

INTRODUCTION

God is aware of and understands all of our thoughts, feelings, and pain. When we are looking for answers, what better person is there to turn to for help than the One who created us and knows all things? While reading through the Holy Bible, I recorded the words God used to speak to my heart concerning the questions and emotions I had while suffering with chronic illnesses.

You may have many of the same questions. My prayer for you is that as you read this book, God will speak to you through His Word. And may He answer your questions and bring you comfort and healing physically, emotionally, and spiritually.

PART ONE

QUESTIONS

CHAPTER 1

IS GOD GOOD?

I will tell of the kindnesses of the LORD, the deeds for which he is to be praised, according to all the LORD has done for us—yes, the many good things he has done for the house of Israel, according to his compassion and many kindnesses.

—Isaiah 63:7 NIV

The LORD is good to those who wait for Him, to the soul who seeks Him.

—Lamentations 3:25 NKJV

The LORD is good, a strong hold in the day of trouble; and he knoweth them that trust in him.

—Nahum 1:7 KJV

For You are not a God who takes pleasure in wickedness; no evil dwells with You.

—Psalm 5:4 NASB

For the LORD is good and his love endures forever; his faithfulness continues through all generations.

—Psalm 100:5 NIV

O give thanks unto the LORD; for he is good: for his mercy endureth for ever.

—Psalm 118:29 KJV

Thou art good, and doest good; teach me thy statutes.

—Psalm 119:68 KJV

Praise the LORD; for the LORD is good: sing praises unto his name; for it is pleasant.

—Psalm 135:3 KJV

The LORD is good to all: and his tender mercies are over all his works.

—Psalm 145:9 KJV

For You, Lord, are good, and ready to forgive, and abundant in mercy to all those who call upon You.

—Psalm 86:5 NKJV

As He was setting out on a journey, a man ran up to Him and knelt before Him, and asked Him, "Good Teacher, what shall I do to inherit eternal life?" And Jesus said to him, "Why do you call Me good? No one is good except God alone."

—Mark 10:17, 18 NASB

I am the good shepherd. The good shepherd lays down his life for the sheep. The hired hand is not the shepherd who owns the sheep. So when he sees the wolf coming, he abandons the sheep and runs away. Then the wolf attacks the flock and scatters it. The man runs away because he is a hired hand and cares nothing for the sheep.

I am the good shepherd; I know my sheep and my sheep know me—just as the Father knows me and I know the Father—and I lay down my life for the sheep. I have other sheep that are not of this sheep pen. I must bring them also. They too will listen to my voice, and there shall be one flock and one shepherd.

—John 10:11–16 NIV

DOES GOD CARE ABOUT ME?

Look at the birds of the air, for they neither sow nor reap nor gather into barns; yet your heavenly Father feeds them. Are you not of more value than they?

—*Matthew 6:26 NKJV*

Come to Me, all who are weary and heavy-laden, and I will give you rest. Take My yoke upon you and learn from Me, for I am gentle and humble in heart, and you will find rest for your souls. For My yoke is easy and My burden is light.

—*Matthew 11:28–30 NASB*

And Jesus stood still, and called them, and said, What will ye that I shall do unto you? They say unto him, Lord, that our eyes may be opened. So Jesus had compassion on them, and touched their eyes: and immediately their eyes received sight, and they followed him.

—*Matthew 20:32–34 KJV*

And Jesus came and spake unto them, saying, All power is given unto me in heaven and in earth. Go ye therefore, and teach all nations, baptizing them in the name of the Father, and of the Son, and of the Holy Ghost: teaching them to observe all things whatsoever I have commanded you: and, lo, I am with you alway, even unto the end of the world. Amen.

—*Matthew 28:18–20 KJV*

Are not five sparrows sold for two copper coins? And not one of them is forgotten before God. But the very hairs of your head are all numbered. Do not fear therefore; you are of more value than many sparrows.

—Luke 12:6, 7 NKJV

When Jesus saw him lying there, and knew that he already had been in that condition a long time, He said to him, "Do you want to be made well?"

—John 5:6 NKJV

When Jesus therefore saw her weeping, and the Jews also weeping which came with her, he groaned in the spirit, and was troubled, and said, Where have ye laid him? They said unto him, Lord, come and see. Jesus wept. Then said the Jews, Behold how he loved him!

—John 11:33–36 KJV

Christ Jesus, who died—more than that, who was raised to life—is at the right hand of God and is also interceding for us.

—Romans 8:34 NIV

Blessed be the God and Father of our Lord Jesus Christ, the Father of mercies and God of all comfort, who comforts us in all our affliction so that we will be able to comfort those who are in any affliction with the comfort with which we ourselves are comforted by God. For just as the sufferings of Christ are ours in abundance, so also our comfort is abundant through Christ.

—2 Corinthians 1:3–5 NASB

But God, who comforts the depressed, comforted us ....

—2 Corinthians 7:6 NASB

But my God shall supply all your need according to his riches in glory by Christ Jesus.

—Philippians 4:19 KJV

Now may our Lord Jesus Christ Himself and God our Father, who has loved us and given us eternal comfort and good hope by grace, comfort and strengthen your hearts in every good work and word.

—2 Thessalonians 2:16, 17 NASB

Humble yourselves therefore under the mighty hand of God, that he may exalt you in due time: casting all your care upon him; for he careth for you.

—1 Peter 5:6, 7 KJV

And God shall wipe away all tears from their eyes; and there shall be no more death, neither sorrow, nor crying, neither shall there be any more pain: for the former things are passed away.

—Revelation 21:4 KJV

Then he blessed Joseph and said, "May the God before whom my fathers Abraham and Isaac walked, the God who has been my Shepherd all my life to this day, the Angel who has delivered me from all harm—may he bless these boys...."

—Genesis 48:15, 16 NIV

Joseph said to his brothers, "I am about to die, but God will surely take care of you and bring you up from this land to the land which He promised on oath to Abraham, to Isaac and to Jacob."

—Genesis 50:24 NASB

And when they heard that the LORD was concerned about them and had seen their misery, they bowed down and worshiped.

—Exodus 4:31 NIV

And when the LORD raised up judges for them, the LORD was with the judge and delivered them out of the hand of their enemies all the days of the judge; for the LORD was moved to pity by their groaning because of those who oppressed them and harassed them.

—Judges 2:18 NKJV

Yea, though I walk through the valley of the shadow of death, I will fear no evil; for You are with me; Your rod and Your staff, they comfort me.

—Psalm 23:4 NKJV

The LORD is near to those who have a broken heart, and saves such as have a contrite spirit.

—Psalm 34:18 NKJV

You number my wanderings; put my tears into Your bottle; are they not in Your book?

—Psalm 56:8 NKJV

Show me a sign for good, that those who hate me may see it and be ashamed, because You, LORD, have helped me and comforted me.

—Psalm 86:17 NKJV

Remember your word to your servant, for you have given me hope. My comfort in my suffering is this: Your promise renews my life.

—Psalm 119:49, 50 NIV

Sing, O heavens; and be joyful, O earth; and break forth into singing, O mountains: for the LORD hath comforted his people, and will have mercy upon his afflicted.

—Isaiah 49:13 KJV

As one whom his mother comforteth, so will I comfort you; and ye shall be comforted in Jerusalem.

—*Isaiah 66:13 KJV*

Then shall the virgin rejoice in the dance, both young men and old together: for I will turn their mourning into joy, and will comfort them, and make them rejoice from their sorrow.

—*Jeremiah 31:13 KJV*

CHAPTER 3

DOES GOD LOVE ME?

For God so loved the world, that he gave his only begotten Son, that whosoever believeth in him should not perish, but have everlasting life.

—John 3:16 KJV

And not only that, but we also glory in tribulations, knowing that tribulation produces perseverance; and perseverance, character; and character, hope. Now hope does not disappoint, because the love of God has been poured out in our hearts by the Holy Spirit who was given to us.

—Romans 5:3–5 NKJV

For I am persuaded, that neither death, nor life, nor angels, nor principalities, nor powers, nor things present, nor things to come, nor height, nor depth, nor any other creature, shall be able to separate us from the love of God, which is in Christ Jesus our Lord.

—Romans 8:38, 39 KJV

For this reason I bow my knees to the Father of our Lord Jesus Christ, from whom the whole family in heaven and earth is named, that He would grant you, according to the riches of His glory, to be strengthened with might through His Spirit in the inner man, that Christ may dwell in your hearts through faith; that you, being rooted and grounded in love, may be able to comprehend with all the saints what is the width and length and depth and height—to know the love of Christ which passes knowledge; that you may be filled with all the fullness of God.

—Ephesians 3:14–19 NKJV

We know love by this, that He laid down His life for us; and we ought to lay down our lives for the brethren.

—1 John 3:16 NASB

In this was manifested the love of God toward us, because that God sent his only begotten Son into the world, that we might live through him.

—1 John 4:9 KJV

Know therefore that the LORD your God, He is God, the faithful God, who keeps His covenant and His lovingkindness to a thousandth generation with those who love Him and keep His commandments;

—Deuteronomy 7:9 NASB

Yes, He loves the people; all His saints are in Your hand; they sit down at Your feet; everyone receives Your words.

—Deuteronomy 33:3 NKJV

Your love, O LORD, reaches to the heavens, your faithfulness to the skies.

—Psalm 36:5 NIV

But I will sing of your strength, in the morning I will sing of your love; for you are my fortress, my refuge in times of trouble. O my Strength, I sing praise to you; you, O God, are my fortress, my loving God.

—Psalm 59:16, 17 NIV

I will give thanks to You, O Lord my God, with all my heart, and will glorify Your name forever. For Your lovingkindness toward me is great, and You have delivered my soul from the depths of Sheol.

—Psalm 86:12, 13 NASB

Satisfy us in the morning with your unfailing love, that we may sing for joy and be glad all our days.

—Psalm 90:14 NIV

For as high as the heavens are above the earth, so great is his love for those who fear him;

—Psalm 103:11 NIV

Oh give thanks to the Lord, for He is good, for His loving-kindness is everlasting.

—Psalm 107:1 NASB

The earth is filled with your love, O Lord; teach me your decrees.

—Psalm 119:64 NIV

O Israel, put your hope in the Lord, for with the Lord is unfailing love and with him is full redemption.

—Psalm 130:7 NIV

The Lord openeth the eyes of the blind: the Lord raiseth them that are bowed down: the Lord loveth the righteous:

—Psalm 146:8 KJV

For whom the Lord loves He corrects, just as a father the son in whom he delights.

—Proverbs 3:12 NKJV

I will mention the lovingkindnesses of the LORD, and the praises of the LORD, according to all that the LORD hath bestowed on us, and the great goodness toward the house of Israel, which he hath bestowed on them according to his mercies, and according to the multitude of his lovingkindnesses.

—Isaiah 63:7 KJV

"But let him who glories glory in this, that he understands and knows Me, that I am the LORD, exercising lovingkindness, judgment, and righteousness in the earth. For in these I delight," says the LORD.

—Jeremiah 9:24 NKJV

Who is a God like You, who pardons iniquity and passes over the rebellious act of the remnant of His possession? He does not retain His anger forever, because He delights in unchanging love. He will again have compassion on us; He will tread our iniquities under foot. Yes, You will cast all their sins into the depths of the sea. You will give truth to Jacob and unchanging love to Abraham, which You swore to our forefathers from the days of old.

—Micah 7:18–20 NASB

CHAPTER 4

DOES THE BIBLE SAY WHY PEOPLE GET SICK AND DIE?

And there was a woman who for eighteen years had had a sickness caused by a spirit; and she was bent double, and could not straighten up at all. When Jesus saw her, He called her over and said to her, "Woman, you are freed from your sickness." And He laid His hands on her; and immediately she was made erect again and began glorifying God.

"And this woman, a daughter of Abraham as she is, whom Satan has bound for eighteen long years, should she not have been released from this bond on the Sabbath day?"

—Luke 13:11–13, 16 NASB

You know of Jesus of Nazareth, how God anointed Him with the Holy Spirit and with power, and how He went about doing good and healing all who were oppressed by the devil, for God was with Him.

—Acts 10:38 NASB

After the same manner also he took the cup, when he had supped, saying, This cup is the new testament in my blood: this do ye, as oft as ye drink it, in remembrance of me. For as often as ye eat this bread, and drink this cup, ye do shew the Lord's death till he come. Wherefore whosoever shall eat this bread, and drink this cup of the Lord, unworthily, shall be guilty of the body and blood of the Lord. But let a man examine himself, and so let him eat of that bread, and drink of that cup. For he that eateth and drinketh unworthily, eateth and drinketh damnation to himself, not discerning the Lord's body. For this cause many are weak and sickly among you, and many sleep.

—1 Corinthians 11:25–30 KJV

And I gave her time to repent of her sexual immorality, and she did not repent. Indeed I will cast her into a sickbed, and those who commit adultery with her into great tribulation, unless they repent of their deeds. And I will kill her children with death. And all the churches shall know that I am He who searches the minds and hearts. And I will give to each one of you according to your works.

—Revelation 2:21–23 NKJV

Now a man named Lazarus was sick. He was from Bethany, the village of Mary and her sister Martha. This Mary, whose brother Lazarus now lay sick, was the same one who poured perfume on the Lord and wiped his feet with her hair. So the sisters sent word to Jesus, "Lord, the one you love is sick."

When he heard this, Jesus said, "This sickness will not end in death. No, it is for God's glory so that God's Son may be glorified through it."

Then Jesus said, "Did I not tell you that if you believed, you would see the glory of God?"

So they took away the stone. Then Jesus looked up and said, "Father, I thank you that you have heard me. I knew that you always hear me, but I said this for the benefit of the people standing here, that they may believe that you sent me."

When he had said this, Jesus called in a loud voice, "Lazarus, come out!" The dead man came out, his hands and feet wrapped with strips of linen, and a cloth around his face.

Jesus said to them, "Take off the grave clothes and let him go."

—John 11:1–4, 40–44 NIV

And as Jesus passed by, he saw a man which was blind from his birth. And his disciples asked him, saying, Master, who did sin, this man, or his parents, that he was born blind? Jesus answered, Neither hath this man sinned, nor his parents: but that the works of God should be made manifest in him.

When he had thus spoken, he spat on the ground, and made clay of the spittle, and he anointed the eyes of the blind man with the clay, and said unto him, Go, wash in the pool of Siloam, (which is by interpretation, Sent.) He went his way therefore, and washed, and came seeing.

—John 9:1–3, 6, 7 KJV

"But if you do not obey Me, and do not observe all these commandments, and if you despise My statutes, or if your soul abhors My judgments, so that you do not perform all My commandments, but break My covenant, I also will do this to you: I will even appoint terror over you, wasting disease and fever which shall consume the eyes and cause sorrow of heart. And you shall sow your seed in vain, for your enemies shall eat it."

—Leviticus 26:14–16 NKJV

And Miriam and Aaron spake against Moses because of the Ethiopian woman whom he had married: for he had married an Ethiopian woman. And they said, Hath the LORD indeed spoken only by Moses? Hath he not spoken also by us? And the LORD heard it. And the anger of the LORD was kindled against them; and he departed. And the cloud departed from off the tabernacle; and, behold, Miriam became leprous, white as snow: and Aaron looked upon Miriam, and, behold, she was leprous.

—Numbers 12:1, 2, 9, 10 KJV

And the men, which Moses sent to search the land, who returned, and made all the congregation to murmur against him, by bringing up a slander upon the land, even those men that

15

did bring up the evil report upon the land, died by the plague before the LORD.

—Numbers 14:36, 37 KJV

If you do not carefully observe all the words of this law that are written in this book, that you may fear this glorious and awesome name, THE LORD YOUR GOD, then the LORD will bring upon you and your descendants extraordinary plagues—great and prolonged plagues—and serious and prolonged sicknesses. Moreover He will bring back on you all the diseases of Egypt, of which you were afraid, and they shall cling to you. Also every sickness and every plague, which is not written in the book of this law, will the LORD bring upon you until you are destroyed.

—Deuteronomy 28:58–61 NKJV

Then the Philistines took the ark of God and brought it from Ebenezer to Ashdod. But the hand of the LORD was heavy on the people of Ashdod, and He ravaged them and struck them with tumors, both Ashdod and its territory.

—1 Samuel 5:1, 6 NKJV

Then David said to Nathan, "I have sinned against the LORD." And Nathan said to David, "The LORD also has put away your sin; you shall not die. However, because by this deed you have given great occasion to the enemies of the LORD to blaspheme, the child also who is born to you shall surely die." Then Nathan departed to his house. And the LORD struck the child that Uriah's wife bore to David, and it became very ill. Then on the seventh day it came to pass that the child died ....

—2 Samuel 12:13–15, 18 NKJV

There is no soundness in my flesh because of Your anger, nor is there any health in my bones because of my sin.

—Psalm 38:3 NKJV

Fools because of their transgression, and because of their iniquities, are afflicted. Their soul abhorreth all manner of meat; and they draw near unto the gates of death.

—Psalm 107:17, 18 KJV

The LORD says, "The women of Zion are haughty, walking along with outstretched necks, flirting with their eyes, tripping along with mincing steps, with ornaments jingling on their ankles. Therefore the Lord will bring sores on the heads of the women of Zion; the LORD will make their scalps bald."

—Isaiah 3:16, 17 NIV

And the LORD God commanded the man, saying, Of every tree of the garden thou mayest freely eat: but of the tree of the knowledge of good and evil, thou shalt not eat of it: for in the day that thou eatest thereof thou shalt surely die.

—Genesis 2:16, 17 KJV

Then to Adam He said, "Because you have listened to the voice of your wife, and have eaten from the tree about which I commanded you, saying, 'You shall not eat from it'; cursed is the ground because of you; in toil you will eat of it all the days of your life. Both thorns and thistles it shall grow for you; and you will eat the plants of the field; by the sweat of your face you will eat bread, till you return to the ground, because from it you were taken; for you are dust, and to dust you shall return."

—Genesis 3:17–19 NASB

Wherefore, as by one man sin entered into the world, and death by sin; and so death passed upon all men, for that all have sinned:

—Romans 5:12 KJV

And as it is appointed unto men once to die, but after this the judgment: so Christ was once offered to bear the sins of many; and unto them that look for him shall he appear the second time without sin unto salvation.

—Hebrews 9:27, 28 KJV

The days of our lives are seventy years; and if by reason of strength they are eighty years, yet their boast is only labor and sorrow; for it is soon cut off, and we fly away.

—Psalm 90:10 NKJV

Man is like a breath; his days are like a passing shadow.

—Psalm 144:4 NKJV

To every thing there is a season, and a time to every purpose under the heaven: a time to be born, and a time to die;

—Ecclesiastes 3:1, 2 KJV

Then Job arose and tore his robe and shaved his head, and he fell to the ground and worshiped. He said, "Naked I came from my mother's womb, and naked I shall return there. The LORD gave and the LORD has taken away. Blessed be the name of the LORD." Through all this Job did not sin nor did he blame God.

—Job 1:20–22 NASB

Before I was afflicted I went astray: but now have I kept thy word.

—Psalm 119:67 KJV

It is good for me that I have been afflicted; that I might learn thy statutes.

—Psalm 119:71 KJV

I know, O LORD, that Your judgments are right, and that in faithfulness You have afflicted me. Let, I pray, Your merciful kindness be for my comfort, according to Your word to Your servant. Let Your tender mercies come to me, that I may live; for Your law is my delight.

—Psalm 119:75–77 NKJV

See, I have refined you, though not as silver; I have tested you in the furnace of affliction.

—Isaiah 48:10 NIV

Not only so, but we also rejoice in our sufferings, because we know that suffering produces perseverance; perseverance, character; and character, hope.

—Romans 5:3, 4 NIV

Consider it all joy, my brethren, when you encounter various trials, knowing that the testing of your faith produces endurance. And let endurance have its perfect result, so that you may be perfect and complete, lacking in nothing.

—James 1:2–4 NASB

And we know that all things work together for good to them that love God, to them who are the called according to his purpose.

—Romans 8:28 KJV

A sound heart is life to the body, but envy is rottenness to the bones.

—Proverbs 14:30 NKJV

A merry heart does good, like medicine, but a broken spirit dries the bones.

—Proverbs 17:22 NKJV

Elisha had become sick with the illness of which he would die. Then Joash the king of Israel came down to him, and wept over his face....

—2 Kings 13:14 NKJV

CHAPTER 5

IS GOD ABLE TO HELP AND HEAL ME?

Our help is in the name of the LORD, who made heaven and earth.

—Psalm 124:8 KJV

Many are the afflictions of the righteous: but the LORD delivereth him out of them all.

—Psalm 34:19 KJV

But I am poor and needy; yet the Lord thinks upon me. You are my help and my deliverer; do not delay, O my God.

—Psalm 40:17 NKJV

How blessed is he who considers the helpless; the LORD will deliver him in a day of trouble. The LORD will protect him and keep him alive, and he shall be called blessed upon the earth; and do not give him over to the desire of his enemies. The LORD will sustain him upon his sickbed; in his illness, You restore him to health.

—Psalm 41:1–3 NASB

God is our refuge and strength, a very present help in trouble.

—Psalm 46:1 NKJV

Surely God is my help; the Lord is the one who sustains me.

—Psalm 54:4 NIV

For You have delivered my soul from death, indeed my feet from stumbling, so that I may walk before God in the light of the living.

—Psalm 56:13 NASB

Blessed be the Lord, who daily bears our burden, the God who is our salvation. God is to us a God of deliverances; and to GOD the Lord belong escapes from death.

—Psalm 68:19, 20 NASB

Because he has set his love upon Me, therefore I will deliver him; I will set him on high, because he has known My name. He shall call upon Me, and I will answer him; I will be with him in trouble; I will deliver him and honor him. With long life I will satisfy him, and show him My salvation.

—Psalm 91:14–16 NKJV

For thou hast delivered my soul from death, mine eyes from tears, and my feet from falling.

—Psalm 116:8 KJV

I lift up my eyes to the hills—where does my help come from? My help comes from the LORD, the Maker of heaven and earth.

—Psalm 121:1, 2 NIV

Fear not, for I am with you; be not dismayed, for I am your God. I will strengthen you, yes, I will help you, I will uphold you with My righteous right hand.

—Isaiah 41:10 NKJV

And the book of the prophet Isaiah was handed to Him. And He opened the book and found the place where it was written, "The Spirit of the LORD is upon Me, because He anointed Me to preach the gospel to the poor. He has sent Me to proclaim release to the captives, and recovery of sight to the blind, to set free those who are oppressed, to proclaim the favorable year of the LORD."

—Luke 4:17–19 NASB

Bless the LORD, O my soul, and all that is within me, bless His holy name. Bless the LORD, O my soul, and forget none of His benefits; who pardons all your iniquities; who heals all your diseases; who redeems your life from the pit; who crowns you with lovingkindness and compassion; who satisfies your years with good things, so that your youth is renewed like the eagle.

—*Psalm 103:1–5 NASB*

And, behold, there was a man which had his hand withered .... Then saith he to the man, Stretch forth thine hand. And he stretched it forth; and it was restored whole, like as the other.

—*Matthew 12:10, 13 KJV*

And behold, there was a certain man before Him who had dropsy. And Jesus, answering, spoke to the lawyers and Pharisees, saying, "Is it lawful to heal on the Sabbath?" But they kept silent. And He took him and healed him, and let him go.

—*Luke 14:2–4 NKJV*

And Jesus went about all the cities and villages, teaching in their synagogues, and preaching the gospel of the kingdom, and healing every sickness and every disease among the people.

—*Matthew 9:35 KJV*

Aware of this, Jesus withdrew from that place. Many followed him, and he healed all their sick, warning them not to tell who he was.

—*Matthew 12:15, 16 NIV*

And Jesus went forth, and saw a great multitude, and was moved with compassion toward them, and he healed their sick.

—*Matthew 14:14 KJV*

When they had crossed over, they came to the land of Gennesaret. And when the men of that place recognized Him, they sent out into all that surrounding region, brought to Him all who were sick, and begged Him that they might only touch the hem of His garment. And as many as touched it were made perfectly well.

—Matthew 14:34–36 NKJV

Then great multitudes came to Him, having with them those who were lame, blind, mute, maimed, and many others; and they laid them down at Jesus' feet, and He healed them.

So the multitude marveled when they saw the mute speaking, the maimed made whole, the lame walking, and the blind seeing; and they glorified the God of Israel.

—Matthew 15:30, 31 NKJV

And it came to pass, that when Jesus had finished these sayings, he departed from Galilee, and came into the coasts of Judea beyond Jordan; and great multitudes followed him; and he healed them there.

—Matthew 19:1, 2 KJV

That evening after sunset the people brought to Jesus all the sick and demon-possessed. The whole town gathered at the door, and Jesus healed many who had various diseases.

—Mark 1:32–34 NIV

Because of the crowd he told his disciples to have a small boat ready for him, to keep the people from crowding him. For he had healed many, so that those with diseases were pushing forward to touch him.

—Mark 3:9, 10 NIV

When they had crossed over, they came to the land of Gennesaret and anchored there. And when they came out of the boat, immediately the people recognized Him, ran through that whole surrounding region, and began to carry about on beds those who were sick to wherever they heard He was. Wherever He entered, into villages, cities, or the country, they laid the sick in the marketplaces, and begged Him that they might just touch the border of His garment. And as many as touched Him were made well.

—Mark 6:53–56 NKJV

Now when the sun was setting, all they that had any sick with divers diseases brought them unto him; and he laid his hands on every one of them, and healed them.

—Luke 4:40 KJV

Yet the news about him spread all the more, so that crowds of people came to hear him and to be healed of their sicknesses.

—Luke 5:15 NIV

Jesus came down with them and stood on a level place; and there was a large crowd of His disciples, and a great throng of people from all Judea and Jerusalem and the coastal region of Tyre and Sidon, who had come to hear Him and to be healed of their diseases; and those who were troubled with unclean spirits were being cured. And all the people were trying to touch Him, for power was coming from Him and healing them all.

—Luke 6:17–19 NASB

At that very time He cured many people of diseases and afflictions and evil spirits; and He gave sight to many who were blind. And He answered and said to them, "Go and report to John what you have seen and heard: the blind receive sight, the lame walk, the lepers are cleansed, and the deaf hear, the dead are raised up, the poor have the gospel preached to them. Blessed is he who does not take offense at Me."

—Luke 7:21–23 NASB

And the people, when they knew it, followed him: and he received them, and spake unto them of the kingdom of God, and healed them that had need of healing.

—Luke 9:11 KJV

And a great multitude followed him, because they saw his miracles which he did on them that were diseased.

—John 6:2 KJV

Then the LORD said to Abraham, "Why did Sarah laugh and say, 'Will I really have a child, now that I am old?' Is anything too hard for the Lord? I will return to you at the appointed time next year and Sarah will have a son."

—Genesis 18:13, 14 NIV

O LORD my God, I cried out to You, and You have healed me.

—Psalm 30:2 NKJV

He makes the barren woman abide in the house as a joyful mother of children. Praise the LORD!

—Psalm 113:9 NASB

The LORD openeth the eyes of the blind: the LORD raiseth them that are bowed down: the LORD loveth the righteous:

—Psalm 146:8 KJV

He healeth the broken in heart, and bindeth up their wounds.

—Psalm 147:3 KJV

Surely our griefs He Himself bore, and our sorrows He carried; yet we ourselves esteemed Him stricken, smitten of God, and afflicted. But He was pierced through for our transgressions, He was crushed for our iniquities; the chastening for our well-being fell upon Him, and by His scourging we are healed.

—Isaiah 53:4, 5 NASB

When evening had come, they brought to Him many who were demon-possessed. And He cast out the spirits with a word, and healed all who were sick, that it might be fulfilled which was spoken by Isaiah the prophet, saying: "He Himself took our infirmities and bore our sicknesses."

—Matthew 8:16, 17 NKJV

… and He Himself bore our sins in His body on the cross, so that we might die to sin and live to righteousness; for by His wounds you were healed.

—1 Peter 2:24 NASB

I will refresh the weary and satisfy the faint.

—Jeremiah 31:25 NIV

Behold, I am the LORD, the God of all flesh: is there any thing too hard for me?

—Jeremiah 32:27 KJV

Then they brought him a demon-possessed man who was blind and mute, and Jesus healed him, so that he could both talk and see.

—Matthew 12:22 NIV

When they came to the crowd, a man came up to Jesus, falling on his knees before Him and saying, "Lord, have mercy on my son, for he is a lunatic and is very ill; for he often falls into the fire and often into the water. I brought him to Your disciples, and they could not cure him." And Jesus answered and said, "You unbelieving and perverted generation, how long shall I be with you? How long shall I put up with you? Bring him here to Me." And Jesus rebuked him, and the demon came out of him, and the boy was cured at once.

—Matthew 17:14–18 NASB

Now when Jesus had crossed over again by boat to the other side, a great multitude gathered to Him; and He was by the sea. And behold, one of the rulers of the synagogue came, Jairus by name. And when he saw Him, he fell at His feet and begged Him earnestly, saying, "My little daughter lies at the point of death. Come and lay Your hands on her, that she may be healed, and she will live." So Jesus went with him, and a great multitude followed Him and thronged Him.

Now a certain woman had a flow of blood for twelve years, and had suffered many things from many physicians. She had spent all that she had and was no better, but rather grew worse. When she heard about Jesus, she came behind Him in the crowd and touched His garment; for she said, "If only I may touch His clothes, I shall be made well." Immediately the fountain of her blood was dried up, and she felt in her body that she was healed of the affliction.

And Jesus, immediately knowing in Himself that power had gone out of Him, turned around in the crowd and said, "Who touched My clothes?" But His disciples said to Him, "You see the multitude thronging You, and You say, 'Who touched Me?'" And He looked around to see her who had done this thing.

But the woman, fearing and trembling, knowing what had happened to her, came and fell down before Him and told Him the whole truth. And He said to her, "Daughter, your faith has made you well. Go in peace, and be healed of your affliction."

While He was still speaking, some came from the ruler of the synagogue's house who said, "Your daughter is dead. Why trouble the Teacher any further?" As soon as Jesus heard the word that was spoken, He said to the ruler of the synagogue, "Do not be afraid; only believe." And He permitted no one to follow Him except Peter, James, and John the brother of James.

Then He came to the house of the ruler of the synagogue, and saw a tumult and those who wept and wailed loudly. When He came in, He said to them, "Why make this commotion and weep? The child is not dead, but sleeping." And they laughed Him to scorn. But when He had put them all out, He took the father and the mother of the child, and those who were with Him, and entered where the child was lying.

Then He took the child by the hand, and said to her, "Talitha, cumi," which is translated, "Little girl, I say to you, arise." Immediately the girl arose and walked, for she was twelve years of age. And they were overcome with great amazement. But He commanded them strictly that no one should know it, and said that something should be given her to eat.

—Mark 5:21–43 NKJV

Then Jesus left the vicinity of Tyre and went through Sidon, down to the Sea of Galilee and into the region of the Decapolis. There some people brought a man to him who was deaf and could hardly talk, and they begged him to place his hand on the man.

After he took him aside, away from the crowd, Jesus put his fingers into the man's ears. Then he spit and touched the man's tongue. He looked up to heaven and with a deep sigh said to him, "Ephphatha!" (which means, "Be opened!"). At this, the man's ears were opened, his tongue was loosened and he began to speak plainly.

Jesus commanded them not to tell anyone. But the more he did so, the more they kept talking about it. People were overwhelmed with amazement. "He has done everything well," they said. "He even makes the deaf hear and the dumb speak."

—Mark 7:31–37 NIV

Then He came to Bethsaida; and they brought a blind man to Him, and begged Him to touch him. So He took the blind man by the hand and led him out of the town. And when He had spit on his eyes and put His hands on him, He asked him if he saw anything. And he looked up and said, "I see men like trees, walking." Then He put His hands on his eyes again and made him look up. And he was restored and saw everyone clearly.

—Mark 8:22–25 NKJV

Now it came to pass, afterward, that He went through every city and village, preaching and bringing the glad tidings of the kingdom of God. And the twelve were with Him, and certain women who had been healed of evil spirits and infirmities— Mary called Magdalene, out of whom had come seven demons, and Joanna the wife of Chuza, Herod's steward, and Susanna, and many others who provided for him from their substance.

—Luke 8:1–3 NKJV

And one of them struck the slave of the high priest and cut off his right ear. But Jesus answered and said, "Stop! No more of this." And He touched his ear and healed him.

—Luke 22:50, 51 NASB

Jesus Christ is the same yesterday and today and forever.

—Hebrews 13:8 NIV

CHAPTER 6

IS GOD COMPASSIONATE, MERCIFUL, AND WILLING TO HEAL?

But when He saw the multitudes, He was moved with compassion for them, because they were weary and scattered, like sheep having no shepherd.

—Matthew 9:36 NKJV

And Jesus went forth, and saw a great multitude, and was moved with compassion toward them, and he healed their sick.

—Matthew 14:14 KJV

And as they departed from Jericho, a great multitude followed him. And, behold, two blind men sitting by the way side, when they heard that Jesus passed by, cried out, saying, Have mercy on us, O Lord, thou son of David. And the multitude rebuked them, because they should hold their peace: but they cried the more, saying, Have mercy on us, O Lord, thou son of David. And Jesus stood still, and called them, and said, What will ye that I shall do unto you? They say unto him, Lord, that our eyes may be opened. So Jesus had compassion on them, and touched their eyes: and immediately their eyes received sight, and they followed him.

—Matthew 20:29–34 KJV

Then a leper came to Him, imploring Him, kneeling down to Him and saying to Him, "If You are willing, You can make me clean." And Jesus, moved with compassion, put out His hand and touched him, and said to him, "I am willing; be cleansed." As soon as He had spoken, immediately the leprosy left him, and he was cleansed.

—Mark 1:40–42 NKJV

And Jesus, when he came out, saw much people, and was moved with compassion toward them, because they were as sheep not having a shepherd: and he began to teach them many things.

—Mark 6:34 KJV

And his mercy is on them that fear him from generation to generation.

—Luke 1:50 KJV

And when He came near the gate of the city, behold, a dead man was being carried out, the only son of his mother; and she was a widow. And a large crowd from the city was with her. When the Lord saw her, He had compassion on her and said to her, "Do not weep." Then He came and touched the open coffin, and those who carried him stood still. And He said, "Young man, I say to you, arise." And he who was dead sat up and began to speak. And He presented him to his mother. Then fear came upon all, and they glorified God, saying, "A great prophet has risen up among us"; and, "God has visited His people."

—Luke 7:12–16 NKJV

But I thought it necessary to send to you Epaphroditus, my brother and fellow worker and fellow soldier, who is also your messenger and minister to my need; because he was longing for you all and was distressed because you had heard that he was sick. For indeed he was sick to the point of death, but God had mercy on him, and not on him only but also on me, so that I would not have sorrow upon sorrow.

—Philippians 2:25–27 NASB

Let us therefore come boldly unto the throne of grace, that we may obtain mercy, and find grace to help in time of need.

—Hebrews 4:16 KJV

As you know, we consider blessed those who have persevered. You have heard of Job's perseverance and have seen what the Lord finally brought about. The Lord is full of compassion and mercy.

—James 5:11 NIV

But You are a God of forgiveness, gracious and compassionate, slow to anger and abounding in lovingkindness; and You did not forsake them.

—Nehemiah 9:17 NASB

Remember, O LORD, Your tender mercies and Your lovingkindnesses, for they have been from of old.

—Psalm 25:6 NKJV

You, O LORD, will not withhold Your compassion from me; Your lovingkindness and Your truth will continually preserve me.

—Psalm 40:11 NASB

The LORD is merciful and gracious, slow to anger, and plenteous in mercy.

—Psalm 103:8 KJV

As a father has compassion on his children, so the LORD has compassion on those who fear him; for he knows how we are formed, he remembers that we are dust.

—Psalm 103:13, 14 NIV

Gracious is the LORD, and righteous; yea, our God is merciful.

—Psalm 116:5 KJV

For the LORD will judge His people, and He will have compassion on His servants.

—Psalm 135:14 NKJV

Therefore the LORD longs to be gracious to you, and therefore He waits on high to have compassion on you. For the LORD is a God of justice; how blessed are all those who long for Him.

—Isaiah 30:18 NASB

"For the mountains may be removed and the hills may shake, but My lovingkindness will not be removed from you, and My covenant of peace will not be shaken," says the LORD who has compassion on you.

—Isaiah 54:10 NASB

This I recall to my mind, therefore have I hope. It is of the LORD's mercies that we are not consumed, because his compassions fail not. They are new every morning: great is thy faithfulness.

—Lamentations 3:21–23 KJV

But though he cause grief, yet will he have compassion according to the multitude of his mercies. For he doth not afflict willingly nor grieve the children of men.

—Lamentations 3:32, 33 KJV

CHAPTER 7

CAN PEOPLE HEAL THE SICK THROUGH THE LORD'S POWER?

And when he had called unto him his twelve disciples, he gave them power against unclean spirits, to cast them out, and to heal all manner of sickness and all manner of disease.

—Matthew 10:1 KJV

Heal the sick, cleanse the lepers, raise the dead, cast out devils: freely ye have received, freely give.

—Matthew 10:8 KJV

And they cast out many devils, and anointed with oil many that were sick, and healed them.

—Mark 6:13 KJV

And these signs will follow those who believe: In My name they will cast out demons; they will speak with new tongues; they will take up serpents; and if they drink anything deadly, it will by no means hurt them; they will lay hands on the sick, and they will recover.

—Mark 16:17, 18 NKJV

Then he called his twelve disciples together, and gave them power and authority over all devils, and to cure diseases. And he sent them to preach the kingdom of God, and to heal the sick.

—Luke 9:1, 2 KJV

And they departed, and went through the towns, preaching the gospel, and healing every where.

—Luke 9:6 KJV

Whatever city you enter, and they receive you, eat such things as are set before you. And heal the sick who are there, and say to them, "The kingdom of God has come near to you."

—*Luke 10:8, 9 NKJV*

Now Peter and John went up together to the temple at the hour of prayer, the ninth hour. And a certain man lame from his mother's womb was carried, whom they laid daily at the gate of the temple which is called Beautiful, to ask alms from those who entered the temple; who, seeing Peter and John about to go into the temple, asked for alms.

And fixing his eyes on him, with John, Peter said, "Look at us." So he gave them his attention, expecting to receive something from them. Then Peter said, "Silver and gold I do not have, but what I do have I give you: In the name of Jesus Christ of Nazareth, rise up and walk." And he took him by the right hand and lifted him up, and immediately his feet and ankle bones received strength. So he, leaping up, stood and walked and entered the temple with them—walking, leaping, and praising God.

And all the people saw him walking and praising God. Then they knew that it was he who sat begging alms at the Beautiful Gate of the temple; and they were filled with wonder and amazement at what had happened to him. Now as the lame man who was healed held on to Peter and John, all the people ran together to them in the porch which is called Solomon's, greatly amazed.

So when Peter saw it, he responded to the people: "Men of Israel, why do you marvel at this? Or why look so intently at us, as though by our own power or godliness we had made this man walk? The God of Abraham, Isaac, and Jacob, the God of our fathers, glorified His Servant Jesus, whom you delivered up and denied in the presence of Pilate, when he was determined to let Him go. But you denied the Holy One and the Just, and asked for a murderer to be granted to you, and killed the

Prince of life, whom God raised from the dead, of which we are witnesses. And His name, through faith in His name, has made this man strong, whom you see and know. Yes, the faith which comes through Him has given him this perfect soundness in the presence of you all."

—Acts 3:1–16 NKJV

Then Peter, filled with the Holy Spirit, said to them, "Rulers and elders of the people, if we are on trial today for a benefit done to a sick man, as to how this man has been made well, let it be known to all of you and to all the people of Israel, that by the name of Jesus Christ the Nazarene, whom you crucified, whom God raised from the dead—by this name this man stands here before you in good health."

—Acts 4:8–10 NASB

"And now, Lord, take note of their threats, and grant that Your bondservants may speak Your word with all confidence, while You extend Your hand to heal, and signs and wonders take place through the name of Your holy servant Jesus."

—Acts 4:29, 30 NASB

The apostles performed many miraculous signs and wonders among the people. And all the believers used to meet together in Solomon's Colonnade. No one else dared join them, even though they were highly regarded by the people. Nevertheless, more and more men and women believed in the Lord and were added to their number. As a result, people brought the sick into the streets and laid them on beds and mats so that at least Peter's shadow might fall on some of them as he passed by. Crowds gathered also from the towns around Jerusalem, bringing their sick and those tormented by evil spirits, and all of them were healed.

—Acts 5:12–16 NIV

And Stephen, full of faith and power, did great wonders and miracles among the people.

—Acts 6:8 KJV

When the crowds heard Philip and saw the miraculous signs he did, they all paid close attention to what he said. With shrieks, evil spirits came out of many, and many paralytics and cripples were healed. So there was great joy in that city.

—Acts 8:6–8 NIV

So Ananias departed and entered the house, and after laying his hands on him said, "Brother Saul, the Lord Jesus, who appeared to you on the road by which you were coming, has sent me so that you may regain your sight and be filled with the Holy Spirit." And immediately there fell from his eyes something like scales, and he regained his sight, and he got up and was baptized; and he took food and was strengthened.

—Acts 9:17–19 NASB

Now it came to pass, as Peter went through all parts of the country, that he also came down to the saints who dwelt in Lydda. There he found a certain man named Aeneas, who had been bedridden eight years and was paralyzed. And Peter said to him, "Aeneas, Jesus the Christ heals you. Arise and make your bed." Then he arose immediately. So all who dwelt at Lydda and Sharon saw him and turned to the Lord.

—Acts 9:32–35 NKJV

And in Lystra a certain man without strength in his feet was sitting, a cripple from his mother's womb, who had never walked. This man heard Paul speaking. Paul, observing him intently and seeing that he had faith to be healed, said with a loud voice, "Stand up straight on your feet!" And he leaped and walked.

—Acts 14:8–10 NKJV

God did extraordinary miracles through Paul. Handkerchiefs and aprons that had touched him were taken to the sick, and their illnesses were cured and the evil spirits left them.

—Acts 19:11, 12 NIV

And it happened that the father of Publius lay sick of a fever and dysentery. Paul went in to him and prayed, and he laid his hands on him and healed him. So when this was done, the rest of those on the island who had diseases also came and were healed.

—Acts 28:8, 9 NKJV

Is anyone among you suffering? Then he must pray. Is anyone cheerful? He is to sing praises. Is anyone among you sick? Then he must call for the elders of the church and they are to pray over him, anointing him with oil in the name of the Lord; and the prayer offered in faith will restore the one who is sick, and the Lord will raise him up, and if he has committed sins, they will be forgiven him. Therefore, confess your sins to one another, and pray for one another so that you may be healed. The effective prayer of a righteous man can accomplish much.

—James 5:13–16 NASB

For to one is given by the Spirit the word of wisdom; to another the word of knowledge by the same Spirit; to another faith by the same Spirit; to another the gifts of healing by the same Spirit; to another the working of miracles; to another prophecy; to another discerning of spirits; to another divers kinds of tongues; to another the interpretation of tongues: but all these worketh that one and the selfsame Spirit, dividing to every man severally as he will.

—1 Corinthians 12:8–11 KJV

Now you are the body of Christ, and each one of you is a part of it. And in the church God has appointed first of all apostles, second prophets, third teachers, then workers of miracles, also those having gifts of healing, those able to help others, those with gifts of administration, and those speaking in different kinds of tongues. Are all apostles? Are all prophets? Are all teachers? Do all work miracles? Do all have gifts of healing? Do all speak in tongues? Do all interpret? But eagerly desire the greater gifts.

—1 Corinthians 12:27–31 NIV

"Arise, go to Zarephath, which belongs to Sidon, and dwell there. See, I have commanded a widow there to provide for you." Now it happened after these things that the son of the woman who owned the house became sick. And his sickness was so serious that there was no breath left in him. Then the LORD heard the voice of Elijah; and the soul of the child came back to him, and he revived. And Elijah took the child and brought him down from the upper room into the house, and gave him to his mother. And Elijah said, "See, your son lives!" Then the woman said to Elijah, "Now by this I know that you are a man of God, and that the word of the LORD in your mouth is the truth."

—1 Kings 17:9, 17, 22–24 NKJV

And when Elisha came into the house, there was the child, lying dead on his bed. He went in therefore, shut the door behind the two of them, and prayed to the LORD. And he went up and lay on the child, and put his mouth on his mouth, his eyes on his eyes, and his hands on his hands; and he stretched himself out on the child, and the flesh of the child became warm. He returned and walked back and forth in the house, and again went up and stretched himself out on him; then the child sneezed seven times, and the child opened his eyes. And he called Gehazi and said, "Call this Shunammite woman." So he called her. And when she came in to him, he said, "Pick up your son."

—2 Kings 4:32–36 NKJV

She said to her mistress, "If only my master would see the prophet who is in Samaria! He would cure him of his leprosy." So he went down and dipped himself in the Jordan seven times, as the man of God had told him, and his flesh was restored and become clean like that of a young boy. Then Naaman and all his attendants went back to the man of God. He stood before him and said, "Now I know that there is no God in all the world except in Israel. Please accept now a gift from your servant."

—2 Kings 5:3, 14, 15 NIV

CHAPTER 8

WHERE CAN I FIND STRENGTH?

Finally, be strong in the Lord and in the strength of His might.

—*Ephesians 6:10* NASB

I can do all things through Christ who strengthens me.

—*Philippians 4:13* NKJV

But the Lord is faithful, and he will strengthen and protect you from the evil one.

—*2 Thessalonians 3:3* NIV

Notwithstanding the Lord stood with me, and strengthened me; that by me the preaching might be fully known, and that all the Gentiles might hear: and I was delivered out of the mouth of the lion.

—*2 Timothy 4:17* KJV

If anyone speaks, he should do it as one speaking the very words of God. If anyone serves, he should do it with the strength God provides, so that in all things God may be praised through Jesus Christ. To him be the glory and the power for ever and ever. Amen.

—*1 Peter 4:11* NIV

Both riches and honor come from You, and You reign over all. In Your hand is power and might; in Your hand it is to make great and to give strength to all.

—*1 Chronicles 29:12* NKJV

Do not be grieved, for the joy of the LORD is your strength.

—Nehemiah 8:10 NASB

I lay down and slept; I awoke, for the LORD sustained me.

—Psalm 3:5 NKJV

I will love thee, O LORD, my strength.

—Psalm 18:1 KJV

The LORD will give strength unto his people; the LORD will bless his people with peace.

—Psalm 29:11 KJV

But the salvation of the righteous is of the LORD: he is their strength in the time of trouble.

—Psalm 37:39 KJV

Cast your burden upon the LORD and He will sustain you; He will never allow the righteous to be shaken.

—Psalm 55:22 NASB

Sing aloud unto God our strength: make a joyful noise unto the God of Jacob.

—Psalm 81:1 KJV

How blessed is the man whose strength is in You, in whose heart are the highways to Zion!

—Psalm 84:5 NASB

The LORD is my strength and song, and is become my salvation.

—Psalm 118:14 KJV

My soul is weary with sorrow; strengthen me according to your word.

—Psalm 119:28 NIV

O LORD, be gracious to us; we long for you. Be our strength every morning, our salvation in time of distress.

—Isaiah 33:2 NIV

Do you not know? Have you not heard? The LORD is the everlasting God, the Creator of the ends of the earth. He will not grow tired or weary, and his understanding no one can fathom. He gives strength to the weary and increases the power of the weak. Even youths grow tired and weary, and young men stumble and fall; but those who hope in the LORD will renew their strength. They will soar on wings like eagles; they will run and not grow weary, they will walk and not be faint.

—Isaiah 40:28–31 NIV

I will seek the lost, bring back the scattered, bind up the broken and strengthen the sick....

—Ezekiel 34:16 NASB

The LORD God is my strength; He will make my feet like deer's feet, and He will make me walk on my high hills.

—Habakkuk 3:19 NKJV

CHAPTER 9

HOW CAN I BE SAVED?

Surely the arm of the LORD is not too short to save, nor his ear too dull to hear. But your iniquities have separated you from your God; your sins have hidden his face from you, so that he will not hear.

—Isaiah 59:1, 2 NIV

For all have sinned, and come short of the glory of God;

—Romans 3:23 KJV

For the wages of sin is death; but the gift of God is eternal life through Jesus Christ our Lord.

—Romans 6:23 KJV

Now after John was put in prison, Jesus came to Galilee, preaching the gospel of the kingdom of God, and saying, "The time is fulfilled, and the kingdom of God is at hand. Repent, and believe in the gospel."

—Mark 1:14, 15 NKJV

Now I make known to you, brethren, the gospel which I preached to you, which also you received, in which also you stand, by which also you are saved, if you hold fast the word which I preached to you, unless you believed in vain. For I delivered to you as of first importance what I also received, that Christ died for our sins according to the Scriptures, and that He was buried, and that He was raised on the third day according to the Scriptures, and that He appeared to Cephas, then to the twelve.

—1 Corinthians 15:1–5 NASB

For God so loved the world that he gave his one and only Son, that whoever believes in him shall not perish but have eternal life.

—John 3:16 NIV

Jesus heard that they had cast him out; and when He had found him, He said to him, "Do you believe in the Son of God?" He answered and said, "Who is He, Lord, that I may believe in Him?" And Jesus said to him, "You have both seen Him and it is He who is talking with you." Then he said, "Lord, I believe!" And he worshiped Him.

—John 9:35–38 NKJV

Jesus said to her, "I am the resurrection and the life. He who believes in me will live, even though he dies; and whoever lives and believes in me will never die. Do you believe this?" "Yes, Lord," she told him, "I believe that you are the Christ, the Son of God, who was to come into the world."

—John 11:25–27 NIV

Then He said to Thomas, "Reach here with your finger, and see My hands; and reach here your hand and put it into My side; and do not be unbelieving, but believing." Thomas answered and said to Him, "My Lord and my God!" Jesus said to him, "Because you have seen Me, have you believed? Blessed are they who did not see, and yet believed." Therefore many other signs Jesus also performed in the presence of the disciples, which are not written in this book; but these have been written so that you may believe that Jesus is the Christ, the Son of God; and that believing you may have life in His name.

—John 20:27–31 NASB

And at midnight Paul and Silas prayed, and sang praises unto God: and the prisoners heard them. And suddenly there was a great earthquake, so that the foundations of the prison were shaken: and immediately all the doors were opened, and every one's bands were loosed. And the keeper of the prison awaking out of his sleep, and seeing the prison doors open, he drew out his sword, and would have killed himself, supposing that the prisoners had been fled. But Paul cried with a loud voice, saying, Do thyself no harm: for we are all here. Then he called for a light, and sprang in, and came trembling, and fell down before Paul and Silas, and brought them out, and said, Sirs, what must I do to be saved? And they said, Believe on the Lord Jesus Christ, and thou shalt be saved, and thy house.

—Acts 16:25–31 KJV

For thus saith the Lord GOD, the Holy One of Israel; In returning and rest shall ye be saved; in quietness and in confidence shall be your strength: and ye would not.

—Isaiah 30:15 KJV

Seek ye the LORD while he may be found, call ye upon him while he is near: let the wicked forsake his way, and the unrighteous man his thoughts: and let him return unto the LORD, and he will have mercy upon him; and to our God, for he will abundantly pardon.

—Isaiah 55:6, 7 KJV

Rid yourselves of all the offenses you have committed, and get a new heart and a new spirit. Why will you die, O house of Israel? For I take no pleasure in the death of anyone, declares the Sovereign LORD. Repent and live!

—Ezekiel 18:31, 32 NIV

That if you confess with your mouth, "Jesus is Lord," and believe in your heart that God raised him from the dead, you will be saved.

—Romans 10:9 NIV

Therefore there is now no condemnation for those who are in Christ Jesus. For the law of the Spirit of life in Christ Jesus has set you free from the law of sin and of death.

—Romans 8:1, 2 NASB

Immediately many gathered together, so that there was no longer room to receive them, not even near the door. And He preached the word to them. Then they came to Him, bringing a paralytic who was carried by four men. And when they could not come near Him because of the crowd, they uncovered the roof where He was. And when they had broken through, they let down the bed on which the paralytic was lying. When Jesus saw their faith, He said to the paralytic, "Son, your sins are forgiven you."

But some of the scribes were sitting there and reasoning in their hearts, "Why does this Man speak blasphemies like this? Who can forgive sins but God alone?" And immediately, when Jesus perceived in His spirit that they reasoned thus within themselves, He said to them, "Why do you reason about these things in your hearts? Which is easier, to say to the paralytic, 'Your sins are forgiven you,' or to say, 'Arise, take up your bed and walk'?

"But that you may know that the Son of Man has power on earth to forgive sins"—He said to the paralytic, "I say to you, arise, take up your bed, and go your way to your house." And immediately he arose, took up the bed, and went out in the presence of them all, so that all were amazed and glorified God, saying, "We never saw anything like this!"

—Mark 2:2–12 NKJV

Then Levi held a great banquet for Jesus at his house, and a large crowd of tax collectors and others were eating with them. But the Pharisees and the teachers of the law who belonged to their sect complained to his disciples, "Why do you eat and drink with tax collectors and 'sinners'?" Jesus answered them, "It is not the healthy who need a doctor, but the sick. I have not come to call the righteous, but sinners to repentance."

—*Luke 5:29–32 NIV*

I said, LORD, be merciful unto me: heal my soul; for I have sinned against thee.

—*Psalm 41:4 KJV*

Heal me, O LORD, and I will be healed; save me and I will be saved, for You are my praise.

—*Jeremiah 17:14 NASB*

PART TWO

RESPONSIBILITIES

CHAPTER 10

CONFESS SINS

When I kept silent, my bones grew old through my groaning all the day long. For day and night Your hand was heavy upon me; my vitality was turned into the drought of summer. Selah.

I acknowledged my sin to You, and my iniquity I have not hidden. I said, "I will confess my transgressions to the LORD," and You forgave the iniquity of my sin. Selah.

—Psalm 32:3–5 NKJV

He that covereth his sins shall not prosper: but whoso confesseth and forsaketh them shall have mercy.

—Proverbs 28:13 KJV

If I regard iniquity in my heart, the Lord will not hear me:

—Psalm 66:18 KJV

If we confess our sins, he is faithful and just to forgive us our sins, and to cleanse us from all unrighteousness.

—1 John 1:9 KJV

CHAPTER 11

FORGIVE OTHERS

And forgive us our debts, as we forgive our debtors.

—Matthew 6:12 KJV

For if you forgive others for their transgressions, your heavenly Father will also forgive you. But if you do not forgive others, then your Father will not forgive your transgressions.

—Matthew 6:14, 15 NASB

And whenever you stand praying, if you have anything against anyone, forgive him, that your Father in heaven may also forgive you your trespasses. But if you do not forgive, neither will your Father in heaven forgive your trespasses.

—Mark 11:25, 26 NKJV

He said to them, "When you pray, say: 'Father, hallowed be your name, your kingdom come. Give us each day our daily bread. Forgive us our sins, for we also forgive everyone who sins against us. And lead us not into temptation.'"

—Luke 11:2–4 NIV

For judgment is without mercy to the one who has shown no mercy. Mercy triumphs over judgment.

—James 2:13 NKJV

CHAPTER 12

CRY OUT IN PRAYER

"And when you are praying, do not use meaningless repetition as the Gentiles do, for they suppose that they will be heard for their many words. So do not be like them; for Your Father knows what you need before you ask Him. Pray, then, in this way: 'Our Father who is in heaven, hallowed be Your name. Your kingdom come. Your will be done, on earth as it is in heaven. Give us this day our daily bread. And forgive us our debts, as we also have forgiven our debtors. And do not lead us into temptation, but deliver us from evil. [For Yours is the kingdom and the power and the glory forever. Amen.]' "

—Matthew 6:7–13 NASB

Then He said to them, "Suppose one of you has a friend, and goes to him at midnight and says to him, 'Friend, lend me three loaves; for a friend of mine has come to me from a journey, and I have nothing to set before him'; and from inside he answers and says, 'Do not bother me; the door has already been shut and my children and I are in bed; I cannot get up and give you anything.' I tell you, even though he will not get up and give him anything because he is his friend, yet because of his persistence he will get up and give him as much as he needs."

—Luke 11:5–8 NASB

Ask, and it shall be given you; seek, and ye shall find; knock, and it shall be opened unto you: for every one that asketh receiveth; and he that seeketh findeth; and to him that knocketh it shall be opened. Or what man is there of you, whom if his son ask bread, will he give him a stone? Or if he ask a fish, will he give him a serpent? If ye then, being evil, know how to give good gifts unto your children, how much more shall your Father which is in heaven give good things to them that ask him?

—*Matthew 7:7–11* KJV

"Again I say to you that if two of you agree on earth concerning anything that they ask, it will be done for them by My Father in heaven. For where two or three are gathered together in My name, I am there in the midst of them."

—*Matthew 18:19, 20* NKJV

Then Jesus told his disciples a parable to show them that they should always pray and not give up. He said: "In a certain town there was a judge who neither feared God nor cared about men. And there was a widow in that town who kept coming to him with the plea, 'Grant me justice against my adversary.'

"For some time he refused. But finally he said to himself, 'Even though I don't fear God or care about men, yet because this widow keeps bothering me, I will see that she gets justice, so that she won't eventually wear me out with her coming!'"

And the Lord said, "Listen to what the unjust judge says. And will not God bring about justice for his chosen ones, who cry out to him day and night? Will he keep putting them off? I tell you, he will see that they get justice, and quickly. However, when the Son of Man comes, will he find faith on the earth?"

—*Luke 18:1–8* NIV

And he said, The things which are impossible with men are possible with God.

—*Luke 18:27* KJV

And whatsoever ye shall ask in my name, that will I do, that the Father may be glorified in the Son. If ye shall ask any thing in my name, I will do it.

—*John 14:13, 14* KJV

If you abide in Me, and My words abide in you, you will ask what you desire, and it shall be done for you.

—*John 15:7 NKJV*

And in that day you will ask Me nothing. Most assuredly, I say to you, whatever you ask the Father in My name He will give you. Until now you have asked nothing in My name. Ask, and you will receive, that your joy may be full.

—*John 16:23, 24 NKJV*

Then Asa called to the LORD his God and said, "LORD, there is no one besides You to help in the battle between the powerful and those who have no strength; so help us, O LORD our God, for we trust in You, and in Your name have come against this multitude. O LORD, You are our God; let not man prevail against You." So the LORD routed the Ethiopians before Asa and before Judah, and the Ethiopians fled.

—*2 Chronicles 14:11, 12 NASB*

And in the thirty-ninth year of his reign, Asa became diseased in his feet, and his malady was very severe; yet in his disease he did not seek the LORD, but the physicians. So Asa rested with his fathers; he died in the forty-first year of his reign.

—*2 Chronicles 16:12, 13 NKJV*

Then they came to Jericho. And as He went out of Jericho with His disciples and a great multitude, blind Bartimaeus, the son of Timaeus, sat by the road begging. And when he heard that it was Jesus of Nazareth, he began to cry out and say, "Jesus, Son of David, have mercy on me!" Then many warned him to be quiet; but he cried out all the more, "Son of David, have mercy on me!" So Jesus stood still and commanded him to be called. Then they called the blind man, saying to him, "Be of good cheer. Rise, He is calling you."

And throwing aside his garment, he rose and came to Jesus. And Jesus answered and said to him, "What do you want Me to do for you?" The blind man said to Him, "Rabboni, that I may receive my sight." Then Jesus said to him, "Go your way; your faith has made you well." And immediately he received his sight and followed Jesus on the road.

—Mark 10:46–52 NKJV

And Hannah answered and said, No my lord, I am a woman of a sorrowful spirit: I have drunk neither wine nor strong drink, but have poured out my soul before the LORD. Wherefore it came to pass, when the time was come about after Hannah had conceived, that she bare a son, and called his name Samuel, saying, Because I have asked him of the LORD.

—1 Samuel 1:15, 20 KJV

In those days Hezekiah was sick and near death. And Isaiah the prophet, the son of Amoz, went to him and said to him, "Thus says the LORD: 'Set your house in order, for you shall die, and not live.'"

Then he turned his face toward the wall, and prayed to the LORD, saying, "Remember now, O LORD, I pray, how I have walked before You in truth and with a loyal heart, and have done what was good in Your sight." And Hezekiah wept bitterly.

Then it happened, before Isaiah had gone out into the middle court, that the word of the LORD came to him, saying, "Return and tell Hezekiah the leader of My people, 'Thus says the LORD, the God of David your father: "I have heard your prayer, I have seen your tears; surely I will heal you. On the third day you shall go up to the house of the LORD. And I will add to your days fifteen years. I will deliver you and this city from the hand of the king of Assyria; and I will defend this city for My own sake, and for the sake of My servant David."'"

Then Isaiah said, "Take a lump of figs." So they took and laid it on the boil, and he recovered.

—2 Kings 20:1–7 NKJV

Have mercy upon me, O LORD; for I am weak: O LORD, heal me; for my bones are vexed.

—Psalm 6:2 KJV

Turn to me and be gracious to me, for I am lonely and afflicted.

—Psalm 25:16 NIV

O LORD my God, I cried unto thee, and thou hast healed me.

—Psalm 30:2 KJV

This poor man cried, and the LORD heard him, and saved him out of all his troubles.

—Psalm 34:6 KJV

Call upon Me in the day of trouble; I shall rescue you, and you will honor Me.

—Psalm 50:15 NASB

I will cry out to God Most High, to God who performs all things for me.

—Psalm 57:2 NKJV

Answer me, O LORD, out of the goodness of your love; in your great mercy turn to me.

—Psalm 69:16 NIV

Incline Your ear, O LORD, and answer me; for I am afflicted and needy. Preserve my soul, for I am a godly man; O You my God, save Your servant who trusts in You. Be gracious to me, O Lord, for to You I cry all day long. Make glad the soul of Your servant, for to You, O Lord, I lift up my soul. For You, Lord, are good, and ready to forgive, and abundant in lovingkindness to all who call upon You. Give ear, O LORD, to my prayer; and give heed to the voice of my supplications! In the day of my trouble I shall call upon You, for You will answer me.

—Psalm 86:1–7 NASB

Hear my prayer, O LORD, and let my cry come unto thee. Hide not thy face from me in the day when I am in trouble; incline thine ear unto me: in the day when I call answer me speedily.

—Psalm 102:1, 2 KJV

I cried with all my heart; answer me, O LORD! I will observe Your statutes. I cried to You; save me and I shall keep Your testimonies. I rise before dawn and cry for help; I wait for Your words.

—Psalm 119:145–147 NASB

I called on Your name, O LORD, from the lowest pit. You have heard my voice: "Do not hide Your ear from my sighing, from my cry for help." You drew near on the day I called on You, and said, "Do not fear!"

—Lamentations 3:55–57 NKJV

Then Daniel returned to his house and explained the matter to his friends Hananiah, Mishael and Azariah. He urged them to plead for mercy from the God of heaven concerning this mystery, so that he and his friends might not be executed with the rest of the wise men of Babylon.

—Daniel 2:17, 18 NIV

From inside the fish Jonah prayed to the LORD his God. He said: "In my distress I called to the LORD, and he answered me. From the depths of the grave I called for help, and you listened to my cry."

—*Jonah 2:1, 2 NIV*

When my soul fainted within me, I remembered the LORD; and my prayer went up to You, into Your holy temple.

—*Jonah 2:7 NKJV*

During the days of Jesus' life on earth, he offered up prayers and petitions with loud cries and tears to the one who could save him from death, and he was heard because of his reverent submission.

—*Hebrews 5:7 NIV*

The sacrifice of the wicked is an abomination to the LORD: but the prayer of the upright is his delight.

—*Proverbs 15:8 KJV*

He will regard the prayer of the destitute, and not despise their prayer.

—*Psalm 102:17 KJV*

In the same way the Spirit also helps our weakness; for we do not know how to pray as we should, but the Spirit Himself intercedes for us with groanings too deep for words; and He who searches the hearts knows what the mind of the Spirit is, because He intercedes for the saints according to the will of God.

—*Romans 8:26, 27 NASB*

Now we know that God does not hear sinners; but if anyone is a worshiper of God and does His will, He hears him.

—*John 9:31 NKJV*

The eyes of the LORD are upon the righteous, and his ears are open unto their cry.

—Psalm 34:15 KJV

The righteous cry out, and the LORD hears, and delivers them out of all their troubles.

—Psalm 34:17 NKJV

I love the LORD, for he heard my voice; he heard my cry for mercy. Because he turned his ear to me, I will call on him as long as I live. The cords of death entangled me, the anguish of the grave came upon me; I was overcome by trouble and sorrow. Then I called on the name of the LORD: "O LORD, save me!" The LORD is gracious and righteous; our God is full of compassion. The LORD protects the simplehearted; when I was in great need, he saved me.

—Psalm 116:1–6 NIV

In my trouble I cried to the LORD, and He answered me.

—Psalm 120:1 NASB

In the day when I cried out, You answered me, and made me bold with strength in my soul.

—Psalm 138:3 NKJV

Call to Me, and I will answer you, and show you great and mighty things, which you do not know.

—Jeremiah 33:3 NKJV

CHAPTER 13

SEEK THE LORD

Glory in His holy name; let the hearts of those rejoice who seek the LORD! Seek the LORD and His strength; seek His face evermore!

—1 Chronicles 16:10, 11 NKJV

If I shut up heaven that there be no rain, or if I command the locusts to devour the land, or if I send pestilence among my people; if my people, which are called by my name, shall humble themselves, and pray, and seek my face, and turn from their wicked ways; then will I hear from heaven, and will forgive their sin, and will heal their land.

—2 Chronicles 7:13, 14 KJV

The LORD also will be a refuge for the oppressed, a refuge in times of trouble. And those who know Your name will put their trust in You; for You, LORD, have not forsaken those who seek You.

—Psalm 9:9, 10 NKJV

I am in pain and distress; may your salvation, O God, protect me. I will praise God's name in song and glorify him with thanksgiving. This will please the LORD more than an ox, more than a bull with its horns and hoofs. The poor will see and be glad—you who seek God, may your hearts live! The LORD hears the needy and does not despise his captive people.

—Psalm 69:29–33 NIV

Let all who seek You rejoice and be glad in You; and let those who love Your salvation say continually, "Let God be magnified."

But I am afflicted and needy; hasten to me, O God! You are my help and my deliverer; O LORD, do not delay.

—Psalm 70:4, 5 NASB

Blessed are they that keep his testimonies, and that seek him with the whole heart.

—Psalm 119:2 KJV

With my whole heart I have sought You; Oh, let me not wander from Your commandments!

—Psalm 119:10 NKJV

"The LORD is my portion," says my soul, "Therefore I have hope in Him." The LORD is good to those who wait for Him, to the person who seeks Him.

—Lamentations 3:24, 25 NASB

For thus says the LORD to the house of Israel: "Seek Me and live; …"

—Amos 5:4 NKJV

HAVE FAITH IN GOD

But without faith it is impossible to please him: for he that cometh to God must believe that he is, and that he is a rewarder of them that diligently seek him.

—Hebrews 11:6 KJV

And a woman who had been suffering from a hemorrhage for twelve years, came up behind Him and touched the fringe of His cloak; for she was saying to herself, "If I only touch His garment, I will get well." But Jesus turning and seeing her said, "Daughter, take courage; your faith has made you well." At once the woman was made well.

—Matthew 9:20–22 NASB

When Jesus departed from there, two blind men followed Him, crying out and saying, "Son of David, have mercy on us!" And when He had come into the house, the blind men came to Him. And Jesus said to them, "Do you believe that I am able to do this?" They said to Him, "Yes, Lord." Then He touched their eyes, saying, "According to your faith let it be to you." And their eyes were opened.

—Matthew 9:27–30 NKJV

And they came to Jericho: and as he went out of Jericho with his disciples and a great number of people, blind Bartimaeus, the son of Timaeus, sat by the highway side begging. And when he heard that it was Jesus of Nazareth, he began to cry out, and say, Jesus, thou son of David, have mercy on me. And Jesus said unto him, Go thy way; thy faith hath made thee whole.

And immediately he received his sight, and followed Jesus in the way.

—*Mark 10:46, 47, 52* KJV

And some men were carrying on a bed a man who was paralyzed; and they were trying to bring him in and to set him down in front of Him. But not finding any way to bring him in because of the crowd, they went up on the roof and let him down through the tiles with his stretcher, into the middle of the crowd, in front of Jesus. Seeing their faith, He said, "Friend, your sins are forgiven you."

"But, so that you may know that the Son of Man has authority on earth to forgive sins,"—He said to the paralytic—"I say to you, get up, and pick up your stretcher and go home." Immediately he got up before them, and picked up what he had been lying on, and went home glorifying God.

—*Luke 5:18–20, 24, 25* NASB

Then as He entered a certain village, there met Him ten men who were lepers, who stood afar off. And they lifted up their voices and said, "Jesus, Master, have mercy on us!" So when He saw them, He said to them, "Go, show yourselves to the priests." And so it was that as they went, they were cleansed. Now one of them, when he saw that he was healed, returned, and with a loud voice glorified God, and fell down on his face at His feet, giving Him thanks. And he was a Samaritan. And He said to him, "Arise, go your way. Your faith has made you well."

—*Luke 17:12–16, 19* NKJV

So Jesus came again to Cana of Galilee where He had made the water wine. And there was a certain nobleman whose son was sick at Capernaum. When he heard that Jesus had come out of Judea into Galilee, he went to Him and implored Him to come down and heal his son, for he was at the point of death. Then Jesus said to him, "Unless you people see signs and wonders, you will by no means believe."

The nobleman said to Him, "Sir, come down before my child dies!" Jesus said to him, "Go your way; your son lives." So the man believed the word that Jesus spoke to him, and he went his way.

And as he was now going down, his servants met him and told him, saying, "Your son lives!" Then he inquired of them the hour when he got better. And they said to him, "Yesterday at the seventh hour the fever left him." So the father knew that it was at the same hour in which Jesus said to him, "Your son lives." And he himself believed, and his whole household.

—John 4:46–53 NKJV

Now a man crippled from birth was being carried to the temple gate called Beautiful, where he was put every day to beg from those going into the temple courts.

Then Peter said, "Silver or gold I do not have, but what I have I give you. In the name of Jesus Christ of Nazareth, walk." Taking him by the right hand, he helped him up, and instantly the man's feet and ankles became strong. He jumped to his feet and began to walk. Then he went with them into the temple courts, walking and jumping, and praising God.

"By faith in the name of Jesus, this man whom you see and know was made strong. It is Jesus' name and the faith that comes through him that has given this complete healing to him, as you can all see."

—Acts 3:2, 6–8, 16 NIV

In Lystra there sat a man crippled in his feet, who was lame from birth and had never walked. He listened to Paul as he was speaking. Paul looked directly at him, saw that he had faith to be healed and called out, "Stand up on your feet!" At that, the man jumped up and began to walk.

—*Acts 14:8–10 NIV*

Now when Jesus had entered Capernaum, a centurion came to Him, pleading with Him, saying, "Lord, my servant is lying at home paralyzed, dreadfully tormented." And Jesus said to him, "I will come and heal him." The centurion answered and said, "Lord, I am not worthy that You should come under my roof. But only speak a word, and my servant will be healed. For I also am a man under authority, having soldiers under me. And I say to this one, 'Go,' and he goes; and to another, 'Come,' and he comes; and to my servant, 'Do this,' and he does it." When Jesus heard it, He marveled, and said to those who followed, "Assuredly, I say to you, I have not found such great faith, not even in Israel!"

Then Jesus said to the centurion, "Go your way; and as you have believed, so let it be done for you." And his servant was healed that same hour.

—*Matthew 8:5–10, 13 NKJV*

So they brought him. When the spirit saw Jesus, it immediately threw the boy into a convulsion. He fell to the ground and rolled around, foaming at the mouth.

Jesus asked the boy's father, "How long has he been like this?"

"From childhood," he answered, "It has often thrown him into fire or water to kill him. But if you can do anything, take pity on us and help us."

" 'If you can'?" said Jesus. "Everything is possible for him who believes."

Immediately the boy's father exclaimed, "I do believe; help me overcome my unbelief!"

When Jesus saw that a crowd was running to the scene, he rebuked the evil spirit. "You deaf and dumb spirit," he said, "I command you, come out of him and never enter him again."

The spirit shrieked, convulsed him violently and came out. The boy looked so much like a corpse that many said, "He's dead." But Jesus took him by the hand and lifted him to his feet, and he stood up.

After Jesus had gone indoors, his disciples asked him privately, "Why couldn't we drive it out?"

He replied, "This kind can come out only by prayer."

—*Mark 9:20–29 NIV*

And Jesus answered saying to them, "Have faith in God. Truly I say to you, whoever says to this mountain, 'Be taken up and cast into the sea,' and does not doubt in his heart, but believes that what he says is going to happen, it will be granted him. Therefore I say to you, all things for which you pray and ask, believe that you have received them, and they will be granted you."

—*Mark 11:22–24 NASB*

Is anyone among you suffering? Then he must pray. Is anyone cheerful? He is to sing praises. Is anyone among you sick? Then he must call for the elders of the church and they are to pray over him, anointing him with oil in the name of the Lord; and the prayer offered in faith will restore the one who is sick, and the Lord will raise him up, and if he has committed sins, they will be forgiven him. Therefore, confess your sins to one another, and pray for one another so that you may be healed. The effective prayer of a righteous man can accomplish much.

—*James 5:13–16 NASB*

Now the God of hope fill you with all joy and peace in believing, that ye may abound in hope, through the power of the Holy Ghost.

—*Romans 15:13 KJV*

And they took offense at Him. But Jesus said to them, "A prophet is not without honor except in his hometown and in his own household." And He did not do many miracles there because of their unbelief.

—Matthew 13:57, 58 NASB

The Jews then gathered around Him, and were saying to Him, "How long will You keep us in suspense? If You are the Christ, tell us plainly." Jesus answered them, "I told you, and you do not believe; the works that I do in My Father's name, these testify of Me. But you do not believe because you are not of My sheep. My sheep hear My voice, and I know them, and they follow Me; and I give eternal life to them, and they will never perish; and no one will snatch them out of My hand. My Father, who has given them to Me, is greater than all; and no one is able to snatch them out of the Father's hand. I and the Father are one."

—John 10:24–30 NASB

"Let not your heart be troubled; you believe in God, believe also in Me. Do you not believe that I am in the Father, and the Father in Me? The words that I speak to you I do not speak on My own authority; but the Father who dwells in Me does the works. Believe me that I am in the Father and the Father in Me, or else believe Me for the sake of the works themselves."

—John 14:1, 10, 11 NKJV

Then He said to Thomas, "Reach your finger here, and look at My hands; and reach your hand here, and put it into My side. Do not be unbelieving, but believing."

—John 20:27 NKJV

CHAPTER 15

TRUST IN GOD AND TAKE REFUGE IN HIM

The LORD is my strength and my shield; my heart trusted in him, and I am helped: therefore my heart greatly rejoiceth; and with my song will I praise him.

—Psalm 28:7 KJV

When I am afraid, I will trust in you. In God, whose word I praise, in God I trust; I will not be afraid. What can mortal man do to me?

—Psalm 56:3, 4 NIV

In God is my salvation and my glory: the rock of my strength, and my refuge, is in God. Trust in him at all times; ye people, pour out your heart before him: God is a refuge for us. Selah.

—Psalm 62:7, 8 KJV

I will say of the LORD, He is my refuge and my fortress: my God; in him will I trust.

—Psalm 91:2 KJV

Ye that fear the LORD, trust in the LORD: he is their help and their shield.

—Psalm 115:11 KJV

Cause me to hear Your lovingkindness in the morning, for in You do I trust; cause me to know the way in which I should walk, for I lift up my soul to You.

—Psalm 143:8 NKJV

Blessed is the man who trusts in the LORD, and whose hope is the LORD.

—Jeremiah 17:7 NKJV

While Jeremiah had been confined in the courtyard of the guard, the word of the LORD came to him: "Go and tell Ebed-Melech the Cushite, 'This is what the LORD Almighty, the God of Israel, says: I am about to fulfill my words against this city through disaster, not prosperity. At that time they will be fulfilled before your eyes. But I will rescue you on that day, declares the LORD; you will not be handed over to those you fear. I will save you; you will not fall by the sword but will escape with your life, because you trust in me, declares the LORD.' "

—Jeremiah 39:15–18 NIV

The king was overjoyed and gave orders to lift Daniel out of the den. And when Daniel was lifted from the den, no wound was found on him, because he had trusted in his God.

—Daniel 6:23 NIV

But let all who take refuge in You be glad, let them ever sing for joy; and may You shelter them, that those who love Your name may exult in You.

—Psalm 5:11 NASB

But I will sing of Your power; yes, I will sing aloud of Your mercy in the morning; for You have been my defense and refuge in the day of my trouble.

—Psalm 59:16 NKJV

But the LORD is my defence; and my God is the rock of my refuge.

—Psalm 94:22 KJV

It is better to take refuge in the Lord than to trust in man. It is better to take refuge in the Lord than to trust in princes.

—*Psalm 118:8, 9 NIV*

But my eyes are upon You, O God the Lord; in You I take refuge; do not leave my soul destitute.

—*Psalm 141:8 NKJV*

Every word of God is flawless; he is a shield to those who take refuge in him.

—*Proverbs 30:5 NIV*

But as for me, I shall sing of Your strength; yes, I shall joyfully sing of Your lovingkindness in the morning, for You have been my stronghold and a refuge in the day of my distress.

—*Psalm 59:16 NASB*

CHAPTER 16

LOVE GOD AND OBEY HIM

And thou shalt love the LORD thy God with all thine heart, and with all thy soul, and with all thy might.

—Deuteronomy 6:5 KJV

Therefore know that the LORD your God, He is God, the faithful God who keeps covenant and mercy for a thousand generations with those who love Him and keep His commandments;

—Deuteronomy 7:9 NKJV

"I call heaven and earth to witness against you today, that I have set before you life and death, the blessing and the curse. So choose life in order that you may live, you and your descendants, by loving the LORD your God, by obeying His voice, and by holding fast to Him; for this is your life and the length of your days, that you may live in the land which the LORD swore to your fathers, to Abraham, Isaac, and Jacob, to give them."

—Deuteronomy 30:19, 20 NASB

Because he has loved Me, therefore I will deliver him; I will set him securely on high, because he has known My name.

—Psalm 91:14 NASB

The LORD is near to all who call upon Him, to all who call upon Him in truth. He will fulfill the desire of those who fear Him; He also will hear their cry and save them. The LORD preserves all who love Him, but all the wicked He will destroy.

—Psalm 145:18–20 NKJV

Unless Your law had been my delight, I would then have perished in my affliction. I will never forget Your precepts, for by them You have given me life.

—Psalm 119:92, 93 NKJV

Trouble and anguish have taken hold on me: yet thy commandments are my delights.

—Psalm 119:143 KJV

Consider how I love Your precepts; revive me, O LORD, according to Your lovingkindness.

—Psalm 119:159 NKJV

Those who love Your law have great peace, and nothing causes them to stumble.

—Psalm 119:165 NASB

Let thine hand help me; for I have chosen thy precepts.

—Psalm 119:173 KJV

My son, do not forget my law, but let your heart keep my commands; for length of days and long life and peace they will add to you.

—Proverbs 3:1, 2 NKJV

If ye love me, keep my commandments.

—John 14:15 KJV

Dear friends, if our hearts do not condemn us, we have confidence before God and receive from him anything we ask, because we obey his commands and do what pleases him. And this is his command: to believe in the name of his Son, Jesus Christ, and to love one another as he commanded us.

—1 John 3:21–23 NIV

And He said, "If you will give earnest heed to the voice of the
LORD your God, and do what is right in His sight, and give ear
to His commandments, and keep all His statutes, I will put
none of the diseases on you which I have put on the Egyptians;
for I, the LORD, am your healer."

—*Exodus 15:26 NASB*

But the mercy of the LORD is from everlasting to everlasting
upon them that fear him, and his righteousness unto children's
children; to such as keep his covenant, and to those that remember his commandments to do them.

—*Psalm 103:17, 18 KJV*

I cry out with my whole heart; hear me, O LORD! I will keep
Your statutes. I cry out to You; save me, and I will keep Your
testimonies. I rise before the dawning of the morning, and cry
for help; I hope in Your word.

—*Psalm 119:145–147 NKJV*

I hope for Your salvation, O LORD, and do Your commandments.
My soul keeps Your testimonies, and I love them exceedingly.

—*Psalm 119:166, 167 NASB*

He who keeps the commandment keeps his soul, but he who is
careless of his ways will die.

—*Proverbs 19:16 NKJV*

Then one of them, which was a lawyer, asked him a question,
tempting him, and saying, Master, which is the great commandment in the law? Jesus said unto him, Thou shalt love the
Lord thy God with all thy heart, and with all thy soul, and with
all thy mind. This is the first and great commandment. And the
second is like unto it, Thou shalt love thy neighbor as thyself.

—*Matthew 22:35–39 KJV*

The conclusion, when all has been heard, is: fear God and keep His commandments, because this applies to every person. For God will bring every act to judgment, everything which is hidden, whether it is good or evil.

—Ecclesiastes 12:13, 14 NASB

But Jeremiah said, "They will not give you over. Please obey the Lᴏʀᴅ in what I am saying to you, that it may go well with you and you may live."

—Jeremiah 38:20 NASB

Then as He entered a certain village, there met Him ten men who were lepers, who stood afar off. And they lifted up their voices and said, "Jesus, Master, have mercy on us!" So when He saw them, He said to them, "Go, show yourselves to the priests." And so it was that as they went, they were cleansed. And He said to him, "Arise, go your way. Your faith has made you well."

—Luke 17:12–14, 19 NKJV

Now a certain man was there who had an infirmity thirty-eight years. When Jesus saw him lying there, and knew that he already had been in that condition a long time, He said to him, "Do you want to be made well?" The sick man answered Him, "Sir, I have no man to put me into the pool when the water is stirred up; but while I am coming, another steps down before me." Jesus said to him, "Rise, take up your bed and walk." And immediately the man was made well, took up his bed, and walked. And that day was the Sabbath. Afterward Jesus found him in the temple, and said to him, "See, you have been made well. Sin no more, lest a worse thing come upon you."

—John 5:5–9, 14 NKJV

As he went along, he saw a man blind from birth. ... he spit on the ground, made some mud with the saliva, and put it on the man's eyes. "Go," he told him, "wash in the pool of Siloam" (this word means Sent). So the man went and washed, and came home seeing.

—John 9:1, 6, 7 NIV

CHAPTER 17

FEAR GOD AND SERVE OTHERS

Ye that fear the LORD, trust in the LORD: he is their help and their shield.

—Psalm 115:11 KJV

The LORD favors those who fear Him, those who wait for His lovingkindness.

—Psalm 147:11 NASB

Do not be wise in your own eyes; fear the LORD and turn away from evil. It will be healing to your body and refreshment to your bones.

—Proverbs 3:7, 8 NASB

The fear of the LORD is the beginning of wisdom, and the knowledge of the Holy One is understanding. For by me your days will be multiplied, and years of life will be added to you.

—Proverbs 9:10, 11 NKJV

The fear of the LORD prolongs life, but the years of the wicked will be shortened.

—Proverbs 10:27 NASB

By humility and the fear of the LORD are riches, and honour, and life.

—Proverbs 22:4 KJV

I know that everything God does will endure forever; nothing can be added to it and nothing taken from it. God does it, so men will revere him.

—Ecclesiastes 3:14 NIV

But for you who revere my name, the sun of righteousness will rise with healing in its wings. And you will go out and leap like calves released from the stall.

—Malachi 4:2 NIV

Then Jesus came and spoke to them, saying, "All authority has been given to Me in heaven and on earth. Go therefore and make disciples of all the nations, baptizing them in the name of the Father and of the Son and of the Holy Spirit, teaching them to observe all things that I have commanded you; and lo, I am with you always, even to the end of the age." Amen.

—Matthew 28:18–20 NKJV

Now He arose from the synagogue and entered Simon's house. But Simon's wife's mother was sick with a high fever, and they made request of Him concerning her. So He stood over her and rebuked the fever, and it left her. And immediately she arose and served them.

—Luke 4:38, 39 NKJV

But when you give a banquet, invite the poor, the crippled, the lame, the blind, and you will be blessed. Although they cannot repay you, you will be repaid at the resurrection of the righteous.

—Luke 14:13, 14 NIV

Blessed be the God and Father of our Lord Jesus Christ, the Father of mercies and God of all comfort, who comforts us in all our affliction so that we will be able to comfort those who are in any affliction with the comfort with which we ourselves are comforted by God.

—2 Corinthians 1:3, 4 NASB

For we are His workmanship, created in Christ Jesus for good works, which God prepared beforehand that we should walk in them.

—Ephesians 2:10 NKJV

Now we exhort you, brethren, warn those who are unruly, comfort the fainthearted, uphold the weak, be patient with all.

—1 Thessalonians 5:14 NKJV

If anyone speaks, he should do it as one speaking the very words of God. If anyone serves, he should do it with the strength God provides, so that in all things God may be praised through Jesus Christ. To him be the glory and the power for ever and ever. Amen.

—1 Peter 4:11 NIV

So you shall serve the LORD your God, and He will bless your bread and your water. And I will take sickness away from the midst of you.

—Exodus 23:25 NKJV

How blessed is he who considers the helpless; the LORD will deliver him in a day of trouble. The LORD will protect him and keep him alive, and he shall be called blessed upon the earth; and do not give him over to the desire of his enemies. The LORD will sustain him upon his sickbed; in his illness, You restore him to health.

—Psalm 41:1–3 NASB

Encourage the exhausted, and strengthen the feeble.

—Isaiah 35:3 NASB

CHAPTER 18

DO NOT WORRY

Therefore I say to you, do not worry about your life, what you will eat or what you will drink; nor about your body, what you will put on. Is not life more than food and the body more than clothing?

—*Matthew 6:25 NKJV*

Therefore do not worry about tomorrow, for tomorrow will worry about itself. Each day has enough trouble of its own.

—*Matthew 6:34 NIV*

But when Jesus heard it, He answered him, saying, "Do not be afraid; only believe, and she will be made well."

—*Luke 8:50 NKJV*

Peace I leave with you, my peace I give unto you: not as the world giveth, give I unto you. Let not your heart be troubled, neither let it be afraid.

—*John 14:27 KJV*

Be anxious for nothing, but in everything by prayer and supplication, with thanksgiving, let your requests be made known to God; and the peace of God, which surpasses all understanding, will guard your hearts and minds through Christ Jesus.

—*Philippians 4:6, 7 NKJV*

Humble yourselves, therefore, under God's mighty hand, that he may lift you up in due time. Cast all your anxiety on him because he cares for you.

—*1 Peter 5:6, 7 NIV*

Fear not, for I am with you; be not dismayed, for I am your God. I will strengthen you, yes, I will help you, I will uphold you with My righteous right hand.

—Isaiah 41:10 NKJV

CHAPTER 19

LISTEN TO AND FOLLOW HIM

Then a cloud appeared and enveloped them, and a voice came from the cloud: "This is my Son, whom I love. Listen to him!"

—Mark 9:7 NIV

He who turns away his ear from listening to the law, even his prayer is an abomination.

—Proverbs 28:9 NASB

Incline your ear and come to Me. Listen, that you may live; and I will make an everlasting covenant with you, according to the faithful mercies shown to David.

—Isaiah 55:3 NASB

"Whether it is pleasant or unpleasant, we will listen to the voice of the LORD our God to whom we are sending you, so that it may go well with us when we listen to the voice of the LORD our God."

—Jeremiah 42:6 NASB

And Jesus answered and said to him, "What do you want Me to do for you?" The blind man said to Him, "Rabboni, that I may receive my sight." Then Jesus said to him, "Go your way; your faith has made you well." And immediately he received his sight and followed Jesus on the road.

—Mark 10:51, 52 NKJV

My sheep hear my voice, and I know them, and they follow me: and I give unto them eternal life; and they shall never perish, neither shall any man pluck them out of my hand.

—John 10:27, 28 KJV

Indeed, He loves the people; all Your holy ones are in Your hand, and they followed in Your steps; everyone receives of Your words.

—Deuteronomy 33:3 NASB

To this you were called, because Christ suffered for you, leaving you an example, that you should follow in his steps. "He committed no sin, and no deceit was found in his mouth." When they hurled their insults at him, he did not retaliate; when he suffered, he made no threats. Instead, he entrusted himself to him who judges justly. He himself bore our sins in his body on the tree, so that we might die to sins and live for righteousness; by his wounds you have been healed. For you were like sheep going astray, but now you have returned to the Shepherd and Overseer of your souls.

—1 Peter 2:21–25 NIV

CHAPTER 20

PRAISE, THANK, AND GLORIFY GOD

Be anxious for nothing, but in everything by prayer and supplication, with thanksgiving, let your requests be made known to God; and the peace of God, which surpasses all understanding, will guard your hearts and minds through Christ Jesus.

—Philippians 4:6, 7 NKJV

By him therefore let us offer the sacrifice of praise to God continually, that is, the fruit of our lips giving thanks to his name.

—Hebrews 13:15 KJV

The LORD is my strength and song, and He has become my salvation; He is my God, and I will praise Him; my father's God, and I will exalt him.

—Exodus 15:2 NKJV

The LORD is my strength and my shield; my heart trusts in him, and I am helped. My heart leaps for joy and I will give thanks to him in song.

—Psalm 28:7 NIV

Why are you in despair, O my soul? And why are you disturbed within me? Hope in God, for I shall again praise Him, the help of my countenance and my God.

—Psalm 43:5 NASB

Sing praises to God, sing praises: sing praises unto our King, sing praises.

—Psalm 47:6 KJV

I am in pain and distress; may your salvation, O God, protect me. I will praise God's name in song and glorify him with thanksgiving. This will please the LORD more than an ox, more than a bull with its horns and hoofs.

—Psalm 69:29–31 NIV

I will praise you, O Lord my God, with all my heart; I will glorify your name forever. For great is your love toward me; you have delivered my soul from the depths of the grave.

—Psalm 86:12, 13 NIV

Be glad in the LORD, you righteous ones, and give thanks to His holy name.

—Psalm 97:12 NASB

Enter into his gates with thanksgiving, and into his courts with praise: be thankful unto him, and bless his name. For the LORD is good; his mercy is everlasting; and his truth endureth to all generations.

—Psalm 100:4, 5 KJV

I will sing unto the LORD as long as I live: I will sing praise to my God while I have my being.

—Psalm 104:33 KJV

Praise ye the LORD. O give thanks unto the LORD; for he is good: for his mercy endureth for ever.

—Psalm 106:1 KJV

Let them give thanks to the LORD for His lovingkindness, and for His wonders to the sons of men!

—Psalm 107:8 NASB

I will give thanks to You, O LORD, among the peoples, and I will sing praises to You among the nations. For Your lovingkindness is great above the heavens, and Your truth reaches to the skies.

—*Psalm 108:3, 4 NASB*

He settles the barren woman in her home as a happy mother of children. Praise the LORD.

—*Psalm 113:9 NIV*

O praise the LORD, all ye nations: praise him, all ye people. For his merciful kindness is great toward us: and the truth of the LORD endureth for ever. Praise ye the LORD.

—*Psalm 117:1, 2 KJV*

I will give you thanks, for you answered me; you have become my salvation.

—*Psalm 118:21 NIV*

Seven times a day I praise You, because of Your righteous judgments.

—*Psalm 119:164 NKJV*

Let my cry come before You, O LORD; give me understanding according to Your word. Let my supplication come before You; deliver me according to Your word. My lips shall utter praise, for You teach me Your statutes. My tongue shall speak of Your word, for all Your commandments are righteousness. Let Your hand become my help, for I have chosen Your precepts. I long for Your salvation, O LORD, and Your law is my delight. Let my soul live, and it shall praise You; and let Your judgments help me.

—*Psalm 119:169–175 NKJV*

Praise the Lord; for the Lord is good: sing praises unto his name; for it is pleasant.

—*Psalm 135:3 KJV*

I will give You thanks with all my heart; I will sing praises to You before the gods. I will bow down toward Your holy temple and give thanks to Your name for Your lovingkindness and Your truth; for You have magnified Your word according to all Your name.

—*Psalm 138:1, 2 NASB*

Every day will I bless thee; and I will praise thy name for ever and ever.

—*Psalm 145:2 KJV*

Praise the Lord! Praise the Lord, O my soul! While I live I will praise the Lord; I will sing praises to my God while I have my being.

—*Psalm 146:1, 2 NKJV*

Sing to the Lord with thanksgiving; sing praises on the harp to our God, who covers the heavens with clouds, who prepares rain for the earth, who makes grass to grow on the mountains.

—*Psalm 147:7, 8 NKJV*

Let everything that has breath praise the Lord. Praise the Lord!

—*Psalm 150:6 NKJV*

Sing to the Lord! Give praise to the Lord! He rescues the life of the needy from the hands of the wicked.

—*Jeremiah 20:13 NIV*

Now when Daniel knew that the document was signed, he entered his house (now in his roof chamber he had windows open toward Jerusalem); and he continued kneeling on his knees three times a day, praying and giving thanks before his God, as he had been doing previously.

—Daniel 6:10 NASB

But I, with a song of thanksgiving, will sacrifice to you. What I have vowed I will make good. Salvation comes from the LORD.

—Jonah 2:9 NIV

A writing of Hezekiah king of Judah after his illness and recovery: "O Lord, by these things men live, and in all these is the life of my spirit; O restore me to health and let me live! It is the living who give thanks to You, as I do today; a father tells his sons about your faithfulness. The LORD will surely save me; so we will play my songs on stringed instruments all the days of our life at the house of the LORD."

—Isaiah 38:9, 16, 19, 20 NASB

"But that you may know that the Son of Man has power on earth to forgive sins"—He said to the man who was paralyzed, "I say to you, arise, take up your bed, and go to your house." Immediately he rose up before them, took up what he had been lying on, and departed to his own house, glorifying God.

—Luke 5:24, 25 NKJV

And there was a woman who for eighteen years had had a sickness caused by a spirit; and she was bent double, and could not straighten up at all. When Jesus saw her, He called her over and said to her, "Woman, you are freed from your sickness." And He laid His hands on her; and immediately she was made erect again and began glorifying God.

—Luke 13:11–13 NASB

Now one of them, when he saw that he was healed, returned, and with a loud voice glorified God, and fell down on his face at His feet, giving Him thanks. And he was a Samaritan. So Jesus answered and said, "Were there not ten cleansed? But where are the nine? Were there not any found who returned to give glory to God except this foreigner?"

—*Luke 17:15–18* NKJV

As Jesus approached Jericho, a blind man was sitting by the roadside begging. Jesus stopped and ordered the man to be brought to him. When he came near, Jesus asked him, "What do you want me to do for you?" "Lord, I want to see," he replied. Jesus said to him, "Receive your sight; your faith has healed you." Immediately he received his sight and followed Jesus, praising God. When all the people saw it, they also praised God.

—*Luke 18:35, 40–43* NIV

One day Peter and John were going up to the temple at the time of prayer—at three in the afternoon. Now a man crippled from birth was being carried to the temple gate called Beautiful, where he was put every day to beg from those going into the temple courts. When he saw Peter and John about to enter, he asked them for money. Peter looked straight at him, as did John. Then Peter said, "Look at us!" So the man gave them his attention, expecting to get something from them.

Then Peter said, "Silver or gold I do not have, but what I have I give you. In the name of Jesus Christ of Nazareth, walk." Taking him by the right hand, he helped him up, and instantly the man's feet and ankles became strong. He jumped to his feet and began to walk. Then he went with them into the temple courts, walking and jumping, and praising God. When all the people saw him walking and praising God, they recognized him as the same man who used to sit begging at the temple gate called Beautiful, and they were filled with wonder and amazement at what had happened to him.

—Acts 3:1–10 NIV

Now to him who is able to do immeasurably more than all we ask or imagine, according to his power that is at work within us, to him be glory in the church and in Christ Jesus throughout all generations, for ever and ever! Amen.

—Ephesians 3:20, 21 NIV

CHAPTER 21

TELL OF HIS WORKS AND WORSHIP HIM

Those who had seen it reported to them how the man who was demon-possessed had been made well. And all the people of the country of the Gerasenes and the surrounding district asked Him to leave them, for they were gripped with great fear; and He got into a boat and returned. But the man from whom the demons had gone out was begging Him that he might accompany Him; but He sent him away, saying, "Return to your house and describe what great things God has done for you." So he went away, proclaiming throughout the whole city what great things Jesus had done for him.

—Luke 8:36–39 NASB

I have not hid thy righteousness within my heart; I have declared thy faithfulness and thy salvation: I have not concealed thy lovingkindness and thy truth from the great congregation.

—Psalm 40:10 KJV

Sing to the LORD, bless His name; proclaim the good news of his salvation from day to day.

—Psalm 96:2 NKJV

Let them sacrifice thank offerings and tell of his works with songs of joy.

—Psalm 107:22 NIV

I will not die, but live, and tell of the works of the LORD.

—Psalm 118:17 NASB

One generation shall praise Your works to another, and shall declare Your mighty acts.

—*Psalm 145:4 NKJV*

Men shall speak of the might of Your awesome acts, and I will declare Your greatness.

—*Psalm 145:6 NKJV*

The living, the living—they praise you, as I am doing today; fathers tell their children about your faithfulness.

—*Isaiah 38:19 NIV*

I will mention the lovingkindnesses of the Lord, and the praises of the Lord, according to all that the Lord hath bestowed on us, and the great goodness toward the house of Israel, which he hath bestowed on them according to his mercies, and according to the multitude of his lovingkindnesses.

—*Isaiah 63:7 KJV*

And he said, Lord, I believe. And he worshipped him.

—*John 9:38 KJV*

And the people believed: and when they heard that the Lord had visited the children of Israel, and that he had looked upon their affliction, then they bowed their heads and worshipped.

—*Exodus 4:31 KJV*

Then Job arose and tore his robe and shaved his head, and he fell to the ground and worshiped. And he said: "Naked I came from my mother's womb, and naked shall I return there. The Lord gave, and the Lord has taken away; blessed be the name of the Lord." In all this Job did not sin nor charge God with wrong.

—*Job 1:20–22 NKJV*

CHAPTER 22

SHOW HUMBLENESS AND KEEP YOUR TONGUE FROM EVIL

But He gives more grace. Therefore He says: "God resists the proud, but gives grace to the humble."

—James 4:6 NKJV

Humble yourselves in the sight of the Lord, and he shall lift you up.

—James 4:10 KJV

Likewise you younger people, submit yourselves to your elders. Yes, all of you be submissive to one another, and be clothed with humility, for "God resists the proud, but gives grace to the humble." Therefore humble yourselves under the mighty hand of God, that He may exalt you in due time, casting all your care upon Him, for He cares for you.

—1 Peter 5:5–7 NKJV

In those days Hezekiah became mortally ill; and he prayed to the LORD, and the LORD spoke to him and gave him a sign. But Hezekiah gave no return for the benefit he received, because his heart was proud; therefore wrath came on him and on Judah and Jerusalem. However, Hezekiah humbled the pride of his heart, both he and the inhabitants of Jerusalem, so that the wrath of the LORD did not come on them in the days of Hezekiah.

—2 Chronicles 32:24–26 NASB

He mocks proud mockers but gives grace to the humble.

—Proverbs 3:34 NIV

This is what the LORD says: "Heaven is my throne and the earth is my footstool. Where is the house you will build for me? Where will my resting place be? Has not my hand made all these things, and so they came into being?" declares the LORD. "This is the one I esteem: he who is humble and contrite in spirit, and trembles at my word."

—Isaiah 66:1, 2 NIV

Why should any living mortal, or any man, offer complaint in view of his sins? Let us examine and probe our ways, and let us return to the LORD.

—Lamentations 3:39, 40 NASB

Come, my children, listen to me; I will teach you the fear of the LORD. Whoever of you loves life and desires to see many good days, keep your tongue from evil and your lips from speaking lies. Turn from evil and do good; seek peace and pursue it.

—Psalm 34:11–14 NIV

My son, give attention to my words; incline your ear to my sayings. Do not let them depart from your sight; keep them in the midst of your heart. For they are life to those who find them and health to all their body. Watch over your heart with all diligence, for from it flow the springs of life. Put away from you a deceitful mouth and put devious speech far from you.

—Proverbs 4:20–24 NASB

The mouth of the righteous is a well of life, but violence covers the mouth of the wicked.

—Proverbs 10:11 NKJV

Reckless words pierce like a sword, but the tongue of the wise brings healing.

—Proverbs 12:18 NIV

A wholesome tongue is a tree of life, but perverseness in it breaks the spirit.

—Proverbs 15:4 NKJV

Pleasant words are a honeycomb, sweet to the soul and healing to the bones.

—Proverbs 16:24 NIV

Death and life are in the power of the tongue: and they that love it shall eat the fruit thereof.

—Proverbs 18:21 KJV

Do not be overly wicked, nor be foolish: why should you die before your time?

—Ecclesiastes 7:17 NKJV

So, remove grief and anger from your heart and put away pain from your body, because childhood and the prime of life are fleeting.

—Ecclesiastes 11:10 NASB

Seek good, not evil, that you may live. Then the LORD God Almighty will be with you, just as you say he is.

—Amos 5:14 NIV

Finally, all of you, live in harmony with one another; be sympathetic, love as brothers, be compassionate and humble. Do not repay evil with evil or insult with insult, but with blessing, because to this you were called so that you may inherit a blessing. For, "Whoever would love life and see good days must keep his tongue from evil and his lips from deceitful speech. He must turn from evil and do good; he must seek peace and pursue it. For the eyes of the Lord are on the righteous and his ears are attentive to their prayer, but the face of the Lord is against those who do evil."

1 Peter 3:8–12 NIV

CHAPTER 23

REJOICE, ACQUIRE WISDOM, AND PURSUE RIGHTEOUSNESS

Rejoice in the LORD, you righteous, and give thanks at the remembrance of His holy name.

—Psalm 97:12 NKJV

Glory in his holy name; let the hearts of those who seek the LORD rejoice.

—Psalm 105:3 NIV

This is the day which the LORD hath made; we will rejoice and be glad in it.

—Psalm 118:24 KJV

I know that there is nothing better for them than to rejoice, and to do good in their lives....

—Ecclesiastes 3:12 NKJV

Indeed, if a man should live many years, let him rejoice in them all, and let him remember the days of darkness, for they will be many.

—Ecclesiastes 11:8 NASB

So teach us to number our days, that we may gain a heart of wisdom.

—Psalm 90:12 NKJV

My son, let them not depart from your eyes—keep sound wisdom and discretion; so they will be life to your soul and grace to your neck.

—Proverbs 3:21, 22 NKJV

For I was my father's son, tender and only beloved in the sight of my mother. He taught me also, and said unto me, Let thine heart retain my words: keep my commandments, and live. Get wisdom, get understanding: forget it not; neither decline from the words of my mouth.

—Proverbs 4:3–5 KJV

Take fast hold of instruction; let her not go: keep her; for she is thy life.

—Proverbs 4:13 KJV

Blessed is the man who listens to me, watching daily at my gates, waiting at the posts of my doors. For whoever finds me finds life, and obtains favor from the LORD; but he who sins against me wrongs his own soul; all those who hate me love death.

—Proverbs 8:34–36 NKJV

Forsake the foolish, and live; and go in the way of understanding.

—Proverbs 9:6 KJV

The teaching of the wise is a fountain of life, turning a man from the snares of death.

—Proverbs 13:14 NIV

The path of life leads upward for the wise to keep him from going down to the grave.

—Proverbs 15:24 NIV

Wisdom is a shelter as money is a shelter, but the advantage of knowledge is this: that wisdom preserves the life of the possessor.

—Ecclesiastes 7:12 NIV

The wages of the righteous bring them life but the income of the wicked brings them punishment.

—Proverbs 10:16 NIV

As righteousness leads to life, so he who pursues evil pursues it to his own death.

—Proverbs 11:19 NKJV

The fruit of the righteous is a tree of life; and he that winneth souls is wise.

—Proverbs 11:30 KJV

In the way of righteousness is life, and in its pathway there is no death.

—Proverbs 12:28 NKJV

The LORD detests the way of the wicked but he loves those who pursue righteousness.

—Proverbs 15:9 NIV

He who pursues righteousness and loyalty finds life, righteousness and honor.

—Proverbs 21:21 NASB

But you, O man of God, flee these things and pursue righteousness, godliness, faith, love, patience, gentleness.

1 Timothy 6:11 NKJV

For He made Him who knew no sin to be sin for us, that we might become the righteousness of God in Him.

—2 Corinthians 5:21 NKJV

CHAPTER 24

CONCLUSION:
WHAT IS THE SOURCE OF LIFE?

"The God who made the world and all things in it, since He is Lord of heaven and earth, does not dwell in temples made with hands; nor is He served by human hands, as though He needed anything, since He Himself gives to all people life and breath and all things; and He made from one man every nation of mankind to live on all the face of the earth, having determined their appointed times and the boundaries of their habitation, that they would seek God, if perhaps they might grope for Him and find Him, though He is not far from each one of us; for in Him we live and move and exist, as even some of your own poets have said, 'For we also are His children.' Being then the children of God, we ought not to think that the Divine Nature is like gold or silver or stone, an image formed by the art and thought of man. Therefore having overlooked the times of ignorance, God is now declaring to men that all people everywhere should repent, because He has fixed a day in which He will judge the world in righteousness through a Man whom He has appointed, having furnished proof to all men by raising Him from the dead."

—Acts 17:24–31 NASB

In the sight of God, who gives life to everything, and of Christ Jesus, who while testifying before Pontius Pilate made the good confession, I charge you to keep this commandment without spot or blame until the appearing of our Lord Jesus Christ, which God will bring about in his own time—God, the blessed and only Ruler, the King of kings and Lord of lords, who alone is immortal and who lives in unapproachable light, whom no one has seen or can see. To him be honor and might forever. Amen.

—1 Timothy 6:13–16 NIV

When Christ, who is our life, shall appear, then shall ye also appear with him in glory.

—Colossians 3:4 KJV

You have granted me life and favor, and Your care has preserved my spirit.

—Job 10:12 NKJV

Who among all these does not know that the hand of the LORD has done this, in whose hand is the life of every living thing, and the breath of all mankind?

—Job 12:9, 10 NKJV

Thus says God the LORD, who created the heavens and stretched them out, who spread forth the earth and that which comes from it, who gives breath to the people on it, and spirit to those who walk on it: "I, the LORD, have called You in righteousness, and will hold Your hand; I will keep You and give You as a covenant to the people, as a light to the Gentiles, to open blind eyes, to bring out prisoners from the prison, those who sit in darkness from the prison house."

—Isaiah 42:5–7 NKJV

But you did not honor the God who holds in his hand your life and all your ways.

—Daniel 5:23 NIV

But he answered and said, It is written, Man shall not live by bread alone, but by every word that proceedeth out of the mouth of God.

—Matthew 4:4 KJV

Because narrow is the gate and difficult is the way which leads to life, and there are few who find it.

—Matthew 7:14 NKJV

The thief does not come except to steal, and to kill, and to destroy. I have come that they may have life, and that they may have it more abundantly.

—John 10:10 NKJV

My sheep hear my voice, and I know them, and they follow me: and I give unto them eternal life; and they shall never perish, neither shall any man pluck them out of my hand. My Father, which gave them me, is greater than all; and no man is able to pluck them out of my Father's hand. I and my Father are one.

—John 10:27–30 KJV

Jesus said to her, "I am the resurrection and the life. He who believes in Me, though he may die, he shall live. And whoever lives and believes in Me shall never die. Do you believe this?" She said to Him, "Yes, Lord, I believe that You are the Christ, the Son of God, who is to come into the world."

—John 11:25–27 NKJV

And many other signs truly did Jesus in the presence of his disciples, which are not written in this book: but these are written, that ye might believe that Jesus is the Christ, the Son of God; and that believing ye might have life through his name.

—John 20:30, 31 KJV

For to me to live is Christ, and to die is gain.

—Philippians 1:21 KJV

Knowing that he which raised up the Lord Jesus shall raise up us also by Jesus, and shall present us with you.

—2 Corinthians 4:14 KJV

I know that my Redeemer lives, and that in the end he will stand upon the earth. And after my skin has been destroyed, yet in my flesh I will see God; I myself will see him with my own eyes—I, and not another. How my heart yearns within me!

—Job 19:25–27 NIV

Therefore do not be ashamed of the testimony of our Lord, nor of me His prisoner, but share with me in the sufferings for the gospel according to the power of God, who has saved us and called us with a holy calling, not according to our works, but according to His own purpose and grace which was given to us in Christ Jesus before time began, but has now been revealed by the appearing of our Savior Jesus Christ, who has abolished death and brought life and immortality to light through the gospel, to which I was appointed a preacher, an apostle, and a teacher of the Gentiles.

—2 Timothy 1:8–11 NKJV

PW

LaVergne, TN USA
23 September 2010
198076LV00001B/55/P